A LETTER
TO
TEACHERS

Vito Perrone

A LETTER TO TEACHERS

Reflections on Schooling and the Art of Teaching

Jossey-Bass Publishers · San Francisco

A LETTER TO TEACHERS
Reflections on Schooling and the Art of Teaching
  by Vito Perrone

Copyright © 1991 by: Jossey-Bass, Inc., Publishers
350 Sansome Street
San Francisco, California 94104

A portion of the poem by Noy Chou in Chapter Five is reprinted with permission of the Massachusetts Advocacy Center. The poem appeared in Denzer, E., and Wheelock, A. *Locked In/Locked Out: Tracking and Placement Practices in Boston Public Schools*. Boston, Massachusetts Advocacy Center, 1990, p. 84.

Manufactured in the United States of America

For sales outside the United States, please contact your local Simon & Schuster International Office.

Jossey-Bass Web address: http://www.josseybass.com

Library of Congress Cataloging-in-Publication Data

Perrone, Vito.

   A letter to teachers : reflections on schooling and the art of teaching / Vito Perrone.
     p. cm. — (The Jossey-Bass education series)
   Includes bibliographical references and index.
   ISBN 1-55542-327-2. — ISBN 1-55542-313-2 (pbk.)
    1. Teaching. 2. Teachers—United States. 3. Education—Philosophy. I. Title.
   II. Series.
   LB1775.P48   1991
   371.1'02—dc20   90–19890

JACKET AND COVER DESIGN BY FIFTH STREET DESIGN

FIRST EDITION
PB Printing   10 9 8 7 6

The Jossey-Bass
Education Series

To Carmel Perrone,
Who Provided Most of the
Encouragement for This Book

Contents

Preface   xi

The Author   xv

1. Toward Large Purposes   1

2. Deciding What to Teach   12

3. Engaging the Students   25

4. The Community and the School   38

5. Valuing Differences   45

6. Evaluating and Grading Student Performance   55

7. Matters of Accountability   68

8. Empowering Teachers   80

9. Refining the Craft of Teaching   97

10.   The Next Generation of Teachers   110

11.   The Importance of Historical Perspective   120

12.   Strengthening Our Commitment to Schools   131

      Bibliography   135

      Index   143

Preface

I have been a teacher most of my life. In the neighborhood in which I grew up, almost all the younger children learned how to play outdoor games from me. This kind of informal teaching continued throughout my high school and college years, extending beyond sports to arts and crafts, literature, reading and writing, and community studies.

My teaching has never stopped. Over the years, I have worked with young children, adolescents, and adults in early childhood settings, elementary and secondary schools, colleges and universities. And for the past twenty-eight years, along with continuing my participation *in* schools, I have been privileged to work directly with large numbers of teachers at all levels of the educational spectrum and in virtually all parts of the United States—in small rural communities and in large urban centers, in settings with all the diversity and range of America's population.

My discussions with teachers have been particularly wide ranging because the agendas have been set primarily *by* teachers. They have involved such issues as curriculum and pedagogy, school structures, materials, social and moral values, and the nature of pluralism and democracy. Reflections on these discussions, along with my direct experience of teaching and learning, provide the base for this extended letter to teachers.

Building this book around a letter matches some of the ways teachers have wanted me to interact with them, essentially providing a context for framing questions that can serve as a foundation for focused discussion and ongoing reflection. The topics I have chosen relate to issues in which teachers have expressed particular interest. They also are among the topics that have personally engaged me for much of my teaching life. During the past year, I have shared various parts of this letter with preservice and inservice teachers in many settings across the country. The material worked among both groups, sparking enormously useful discussion.

In this letter, I have not always differentiated between elementary and secondary schools. Certainly there are developmental considerations that need always to be acknowledged. Still, I believe the issues I raise have meaning at both levels.

There is occasional overlap of ideas in the text. In part, this suggests the artificial nature of organizing around separate topics. I view education in holistic terms, with almost every issue, every subject matter, being connected. In this respect, though the book is organized around chapters, it should be seen as one long, connected statement.

One last comment about my approach: I have made little reference to the many shifting interests that currently surround schools—not because they are unimportant but because they are not the central concerns of teachers in their day-to-day work with students. For example, while shared decision making in regard to school-site management and the "restructuring of schools" fills the educational literature, it is in most respects a political and technical formulation. Shared decision making in these terms may well contribute to improved schools—and I support such directions—but it is not related to the deepest concerns teachers have for their work with children and young people. Professional development schools are also discussed with regularity in the literature, and I am deeply involved in such school–university partnerships; but, once more, this is not central to most teachers as they reflect on their day-to-day lives in the classroom. I also acknowledge that my focus of attention is heavily in the direction of individual teachers, but that is, to a large degree, the nature of the "letter" format. I affirm the essential nature of collective inquiry and action, but the building of more powerful schools must begin, after all, with the work and commitment of individual teachers.

The extended letter is developed around twelve chapters. "Toward Large Purposes" places teachers' work in philosophical as well as pedagogical and curricular perspective, essentially asking a series of why questions. "Deciding What to Teach" reaffirms the belief that teachers need to be central decision makers about curriculum as it unfolds in their own classrooms. It also provides a basis for such decision making. "Engaging the Students" gives attention to beginning points, interesting materials, pedagogical approaches, and generative content. "The Community and the School" advocates a more powerful connection between schools and the diverse resources that exist beyond schools. "Valuing Differences" asks that teachers expand their thinking about the changing demographic patterns in our schools, as well as about curricular and organizational patterns that are supportive of differences. "Evaluating and Grading Student Performance" addresses an area of teaching and learning that has long perplexed teachers, offering ways of rethinking the process. "Matters of Accountability" is related to some of the demands for classroom and schoolwide evaluation, providing directions that go beyond standardized tests. "Empowering Teachers" is a plea for greater authority among teachers, a base for a larger understanding of professionalism. Closely aligned with it is "Refining the Craft of Teaching," which focuses on activities oriented toward enlarging teacher authoritativeness and creating an ethos of teacher reflection. "The Next Generation of Teachers" considers the critical role of teachers in recruiting and preparing the next generation of teachers. And "The Importance of Historical Perspective" is a plea to place our ongoing work within a larger time frame and understand more fully how our current educational conceptions have developed. Finally, "Strengthening Our Commitment to Schools" connects the full text to the challenges that confront teachers and schools as they face a new century.

My hope is that teachers in various settings will find ways to read the book together, to use the letter as a starting point for their own reflections on teaching and learning in the schools. Only when teachers themselves assume the dominant position in regard to issues of teaching and learning in their classrooms, and begin to speak more broadly and authoritatively on matters of education, will we see significant improvement.

Cambridge, Massachusetts   Vito Perrone
December 1990

The Author

VITO PERRONE is a faculty member of the Harvard Graduate School of Education, where he is also director of programs in Teacher Education and chair of the Teaching, Curriculum, and Learning Environments Program. In addition, he is a senior fellow at the Carnegie Foundation for the Advancement of Teaching. Perrone has written extensively about such issues as educational equity, curriculum, progressivism in education, and testing and evaluation. His most recent book, *Working Papers: Reflections on Teachers, Schools, and Communities,* was published in 1989. He has been a public school teacher, a university professor of history, education, and peace studies (University of North Dakota), and dean of the New School and of the Center for Teaching and Learning (both at the University of North Dakota). He serves as coordinator of the North Dakota Study Group on Evaluation and is actively engaged in the life of elementary and secondary schools.

A LETTER
TO
TEACHERS

One

Toward Large Purposes

We are often asked about our purposes (though the word "goals" is more typically used). Yet we don't often engage in serious discussion about purposes, those guiding principles that inform our teaching practices, curriculum patterns, organizational structures, and relationships with students and their parents. They are not fully enough within our consciousness as the source of our work. But they must be. When large purposes lose their centrality, schools tend to drift, forfeiting their independence and their educational and social power. I believe we know this intuitively, yet there is a reluctance to pursue serious questions about purposes. It may be that such discussions appear too philosophical, too abstract, too far removed from the daily tasks of schools. They needn't be removed; such discussions are foundational, times to focus on *first things.*

How should we begin to think about large purposes? Whether we consider the present or the future, education at its best is first and foremost a moral and intellectual endeavor, always beginning with children and young people and their intentions and needs. By and large, though, we tend, in too many of our schools, to be more attentive to technical than moral and intellectual directions. Rather than *education at its best,* we are more often preoccupied with simply getting through the days and weeks.

1

There is, it seems, more concern about whether children learn the mechanics of reading and writing than grow to love reading and writing; learn *about* democratic practice rather than have practice in democracy; hear about knowledge, essentially being in settings where knowledge is dispensed, rather than gain experience in personally constructing knowledge; engage in competition rather than learn the power of cooperation and collaborative thought; see the world narrowly, simple and ordered, rather than broad, complex, and uncertain; and come to accept the vested authority that exists around them in organizational structures and text rather than being helped to challenge such authority, able to bring a healthy skepticism to the world. Further, the belief that art and music—the esthetic aspects of life—call for a special talent and are, therefore, open only to a few rather than being fully accessible to all is to ensure an uninspiring education, one that will surely miss too many of the moral and intellectual imperatives that surround children and young people.

In regard to the arts, their limited presence in most schools is clearly symbolic of how fully technical formulations have come to dominate school practice. There was a time when easels could be found in most classrooms through grade three, in some settings through grade six. They are virtually gone, no longer common even in kindergarten. Why aren't the arts central to every child's education, seen as a critical bond linking math, science, social studies, and literature? How can we be serious about learning and say there isn't time for the arts? I have cited the arts as they are so visibly lacking and at their best so *untechnical*.

What ought to guide us as we consider the schools in relation to large purposes? Very little of what I offer will be new, but possibly in the restating there will be some renewed basis for reflection and action in intellectual and moral rather than technical terms.

What we know most about children and young people is that they are *always* learning. That is their nature. As they touch the earth, observe the culture that surrounds them, listen to stories, and speak, they are achieving a personal relationship with the world, gaining what Jean Piaget calls a balance between changing the world and changing themselves.

If we kept such a view about children and young people constantly before us, we wouldn't be so quick to assume clinical approaches to education, approaches so full of labels. We would put our energy into seeking our students' strengths and not their deficits. Failing to begin with the natural strengths and energy of children and young people as our starting point is to limit the possibilities, to ensure an education with too little power. To paraphrase John Dewey, do we fit the child to the school or make the school fit the child? It might be interesting to engage that question fully again and see where we are. I believe that schools almost everywhere have come to overshadow the child.

In this regard, we are called increasingly in the schools to see our world through a lens of economic competitiveness, the latest of the public imperatives. Today, the focus is on Japan and Germany, with countries such as Korea, Taiwan, China, Singapore, and Brazil close at hand. We need educational settings that fully challenge young people, that provide the skills and understandings that generate ongoing learning both in the schools and in the world. We must want for our children and young people, wherever they are, the best education we can imagine. But placing so much stress on economic competitiveness—stronger math and science programs to *win the war* of technology, for example—is distractive, even as it is distressingly accepted by schools of all kinds. It takes too much away from the students themselves, the immediacy of their educational interests and needs. In its extreme forms, this position looks *beyond* the students, right past them, as if they weren't there. Moreover, such an approach too often prevents us from seeing the world as fully connected, its peoples having mutual needs, growth everywhere being something to rejoice about. And it also easily becomes too instrumental.

The zero-sum formulations associated with competition—gains in Japan meaning necessary losses in the United States—are also self-defeating. Representing the world in these terms causes us to minimize the inequities that currently exist and the imperatives to work actively toward their redress. Is hunger in Africa acceptable? Is the burden of debt carried by Brazil, Peru, Mexico, Nigeria, and Poland their just due? Is that where competitiveness leads?

To speak of economic competitiveness in relation to the world also has an impact at the micro-level of the classroom. Must our goal in the schools also be rooted in a similar competition? Is that how we should define "getting ready for the real world"? Or can cooperation be a principal objective? What are some of the ways to think about this? Shall we, for example, track or not track students? Provide challenge for some and limits for others? Perpetuate inequities or work toward their eradication? Clutter our discourse with labels that pit students against each other, by race, or class, or perceptions of intelligence? Shall we accept the message of test scores or go beyond them? How many of us have seriously challenged the various ways schools separate students? Do we speak about the inequities in the world and ignore those that exist in our schools? In this regard, the inequities tend to be large—and they are growing larger.

We have more than enough to do to create for children and young people genuine communities of learning. Framing our work in terms of competition won't help us do particularly well the first things, the human things.

In relation to the human things, what if we spent time on the question, *What do we most want our students to come to understand as a result of their schooling?* "Reading and writing" might be a quick response, but is this enough? What if our students learn to read and write but don't like to and don't? What if they don't read the newspapers and magazines, or can't find beauty in a poem or love story? Don't see some of *Romeo and Juliet* in their own lives? What if they don't go as adults to artistic events, don't listen to a broad range of music, aren't optimistic about the world and their place in it, don't notice the trees and the sunset, don't look at the stars, are indifferent to older citizens, don't participate in politics or community life, aren't prepared for the responsibility of parenthood, don't have a vision of themselves as thoughtful mothers and fathers, and are physically and psychologically abusive to themselves? And what if they can locate the Republic of South Africa but don't know anything about apartheid and can't feel the pain associated with it? Know about hunger, and collectively waste tons of food each day?

We often speak about children and young people in our society as "the future." What do we imply by such a belief? Preservation, or change? Ensuring that children and young people can live in the world as it is, or ensuring the skills, knowledge, and dispositions that will enable them to *change* the world, to construct on their terms new possibilities? How we think about that will say a lot about what we do in our schools, the ideas we explore, the questions we raise, the books we read, the experiences we provide.

To raise such questions is, of course, to imply the need to keep large hopes before us, to make use of a language and ideals that inspire us beyond our current practices. To those who worry about large hopes serving as guides (and I meet many who are concerned about this), I offer Alfred North Whitehead's belief that "when ideals have sunk to the level of practice, the result is stagnation" (Whitehead, [1929] 1959). Carlos Fuentes, Mexican novelist and diplomat, phrased it differently but also powerfully: "We say justice, we say development, we say democracy. Words won't bring them, but without the words, they will never exist" (Fuentes, 1986, p. 16). Not placing our work within this broader framework, not viewing it as a step toward fuller possibilities is to ensure that what we do will decline in its potency. Because I see this as such an important point, I offer several additional entries—essentially corroboration. Thomas Merton, for example, wrote: "The biggest human temptation is to settle for too little" (in Madlock, 1989, p. 13). And Anton Chekhov offered, "Man is what he believes" (in Madlock, 1989, p. 14), a viewpoint that relates closely to Erich Heller's often quoted statement: "Be careful how you define the world, it is like that" (Heller, 1959, p. 205). In a similar vein, Italo Calvino, one of the world's best storytellers, wrote, "Literature remains alive only if we set ourselves immeasurable goals, far beyond all hope of achievement. Only if poets and writers set themselves tasks that no one else dares to imagine will literature continue to have a function" (Calvino, 1988, p. i). In this sense, teachers need to be like these poets and writers.

In relation to the issue of large hopes, Jean Piaget argued that the principal goal of education in the schools should be the creation of "men and women who are capable of doing new things, not simply repeating what other generations have done—men and women who are creative, inventive and discoverers . . . who can be critical, can verify, and not accept everything they are offered" (in Greene, 1978, p. 80). Thomas Jefferson expressed a similar view about the purposes of public education and life in American society, the understanding that each generation must establish its own revolution. And one can't read Martin Luther King's "I Have a Dream" speech without comprehending the same important point. Why shouldn't the discourse in our schools be more consonant with such an inspiring spirit?

I ask often in this regard, are our children being provided a basis for active participation in the life of their communities? Do they understand the problems and the need to work toward solutions? Are they, in other words, learning the meaning of social responsibility, of citizenship?

If we aren't clear about such questions, keeping them in mind with everything we do, making them a part of our ongoing discourse, we tend to fill our schools with contradictions—and these contradictions only foster cynicism and limited support, hardly the basis for making schools the centers for inquiry, authority, and change they need to be.

I'll offer two vignettes that are related. I could present many more. You will have similar examples from which to draw, to raise to a fuller consciousness.

At a 1986 Peace Studies Symposium at the University of North Dakota, Brian Petkau (1982), a Canadian teacher, presented *A Prairie Puzzle,* a personal statement about the presence of nuclear missiles across the North Dakota landscape and the danger to human life they represent. Several freshman students in the audience expressed considerable anger about how little they knew. They asked why they hadn't learned more about the missile fields, the kinds of weapons that existed and something about their control mechanisms, the cost of these weapons, and, they stressed, their potential as targets. By not making the nuclear arms in North Dakota, or in the country, or in the world, a matter of serious study, what kinds of values were their schools expressing? Were students being prepared for active citizenship?

The second vignette is a more positive entry into citizenship. In Revere, Massachusetts, the principal of an all-white, fully English-speaking school, upon learning several years ago that close to two hundred Cambodian children would be in the school in the fall, started a process aimed at inclusion and social learning of a large sort. The principal and teachers decided that it was critical for everyone in the school—children, teachers, custodians, secretaries, lunchroom workers—to know who these Cambodian children were, where they had come from, and why they were coming to Revere. *Getting Ready for the Cambodian Children* became the full curriculum for several months, the basis for all studies. The train of normal coverage was stopped. Those in the school community learned how to speak to the Cambodian children and also gained considerable knowledge about their cultural patterns as well as their suffering. As part of their preparation, they learned about prejudice and the harm that prejudice brings to people who are different. They also learned how prejudice disrupts communities—whether schools or neighborhoods or cities. Their learning had meaning, and it made a visible difference. It grew out of important social values and commitments related to equity, justice, respect for others, and human dignity, and a willingness to make decisions surrounding such values and commitments. In the world of schools, it was an unusual response. It ought to be the *usual*. Such entries into the world should constitute a large share of the curriculum.

I realize that these two stories and their import border on the political as well as the moral. While there are many pressures to keep such values out of the curriculum, to stay instead close to the technical, the schools would do better to address such issues more directly. They are always present but are most often not acknowledged.

Robert Bellah and his associates in their popular *Habits of the Heart* (Bellah and others, 1985) suggest in this regard that adults are having increasing difficulty explaining their commitments to their children. But children and young people need to know that their parents and teachers have important values. Those beliefs and values come through in many ways. What kinds of values do we present as educators? How do we express caring deeply about the students? About the society? How do we act out our citizenship, show our love for learning? Do we display an ongoing inquisitiveness about the world—how it works and why? Are we critical? Do we seek alternative explanations? Do we ask often about events being examined? What do they mean and why should it matter? Do we engage each other about such things?

Friedrich Froebel, a theoretical and practical giant in the

early childhood field, used the garden metaphor extensively in his writing about children—that sense of unfolding, blooming, and flowering. His metaphor is worth reflecting on.

Experiences do, as Froebel suggested (Froebel, [1895] 1974), build on each other; the more significant they are, the larger their potential for being fully educative, fully generative. Conversely, the less powerful they are, the smaller their overall potential. While each stage of life, each experience, is important in its own right, each is also integrally connected to what precedes and follows it. Learning is never about isolated acts. Such an understanding should cause us to ask always about the continuities between the experience and content of our various levels of schooling and the importance of returning at each level to earlier themes, even texts, as well as not closing off ideas and areas of knowledge being explored beyond a particular level. Is it possible, for example, to go to the Chicago Museum of Natural History too many times? To the Smithsonian too many times? To reread particular books too many times? To revisit Martin Luther King's life too many times? Or Dorothy Day's? Everywhere, though, I hear primary children told: "You don't want to read that book again" or "You will learn about that when you get to the fifth grade." Analogous refrains are replayed often along the schooling track. That, by the way, is one of the means by which difficult questions are set aside.

Further, such understandings about continuities should help us understand what we lose, in fact close off, when we consider curriculum narrowly and in terms of isolated, disconnected studies. Separating learning, as we tend to do, typically leads to less understanding, not more. Can we possibly get intensity with six or seven separate, generally unrelated, nonthematic subject matters a day? When we feel we must get through everything so quickly? We often lament about the poor quality of children's work but don't typically work long enough at anything to ensure it is of high quality. How many of us do our best writing when we are provided ten minutes to complete the task? Or thirty minutes? Or a day? What do we really expect from our students?

Herman Horne, writing in 1917 about the need for teachers to be more like artists, described a teacher who never had the tidiest workshop but "her job is the neatest in the end because students come to deep understandings and complete work they can honor. And while her methods are roundabout and slow moving, what she gives her pupils more than compensates for the length of the route taken" (Horne, 1917, p. xi). He offers a good response to the current admonitions about "time on task" and "coverage."

Returning to the question of large purposes, if we saw the development of active inquirers as a major goal, much that now exits—workbooks and textbooks, predetermined curriculum, reductionism, teaching to tests—would, I believe, begin to fade. Teachers would be free to address the world, to make living in the world a larger part of the curriculum.

Taking such a formulation seriously also means being more attentive to students' inclinations and what they value, what they truly care about. To do otherwise, Patricia Carini suggests, is "to rest content with the appearance of knowledge and forfeit all pretense of educating responsible thinkers, capable of forming opinions and taking actions" (Carini, 1986, p. 23). It is "the appearance of knowledge" that tends to dominate our schools.

It is out of this personal knowledge that bridges to extended learning are constructed. An education that builds bridges, that makes fuller learning more possible, that expands a young person's potential for independence is, in today's terms, an "empowering education." That is a goal worth striving for. And it is a goal that is possible.

Another way to conceptualize continuities and bridges, keeping learning possibilities open, is to consider, as philosopher Mary Warnock puts it, that "the cultivation of imagination . . . should be our chief aim in education" (Lazerson and others, 1985, p. 70). Imagination is in essence a perspective, a way of seeing connections and meanings beyond the routine and the commonplace. Such a perspective demands a curriculum that truly challenges young people, that is laden with questions and multiple possibilities for entry and for active learning. It suggests, as well, time to observe, sit, think, and rework ideas.

To give consideration to imagination also calls upon us to think again about questions of certainty and uncertainty with regard to knowledge, the content of the classroom. Jay Featherstone (1988) suggests that the learning metaphor embedded in Mark

Twain's *Life on the Mississippi,* with the river always shifting, needing to be understood with a high degree of tentativeness, might be helpful. There is a virtue in keeping ideas alive, in keeping their complexity fully in view.

In this regard, Tolstoy noted on the basis of his work with peasant children: "To the teacher, the simplest and most general appears the easiest, whereas for a pupil only the complex and the living appears easy—only that which demands interpretation and provokes thought is easy" (Tolstoy, [1862] 1967, p. 289). Like Featherstone's understanding of Mark Twain's education, Tolstoy viewed ambiguity and uncertainty not as something to remedy, but as the soil for deep learning. We would do well to keep such a perspective in mind. The simple and the certain don't lead to a powerful education in our contemporary age. They are not paths for constructing a democratic society. And they don't provide a basis for optimism about the world.

Paul Fussell in *The Great War and Modern Memory* (1975) suggests that World War I permanently ended our national sense of optimism. That enlarged social, political, and economic optimism that was beginning to emerge before the Great War needs reconstruction. There is a need for new understandings that the world, however defined, is not static, that change is possible, and that change demands a personal and collective investment. An education of consequence ought to encourage such understandings.

I think often these days about Anne O'Hare MacCormick's remark after the signing of the Munich Treaty in the fall of 1938: "All the things are happening that could never happen" (Lean, 1968, p. xii). Bringing her comment into the present and in a different circumstance, who would ever have imagined the changes in the Soviet Union, in Eastern Europe, in South Africa. In these places, all the things are happening that could never happen. New possibilities indeed exist. That understanding should guide us.

Eleanor Duckworth, a former Piaget collaborator and Harvard faculty member, provides us with yet another way to think about purposes. She equates the essence of intellectual development to "the having of wonderful ideas," those occasions when a student, on his or her own, comes to understand a relationship or how something works. Duckworth reminds us: "There is no difference between wonderful ideas which many people have already had and wonderful ideas which nobody has happened on before . . . in each case, it is a matter of making new connections between things already mastered" (Duckworth, 1987, p. 231). Thus, $E = mc^2$ is a lot like a child's understanding that trees and houses are related. I like that idea very much.

A school committed to supporting "the having of wonderful ideas" is establishing for itself the goal of getting all young people as close as possible to their upper limits of learning potentialities. As it is, most don't come very close to that upper limit. The expectations aren't high enough, the environments for learning are too sparse, the questions asked are too small, and the resources too limited. Inevitably, as well, powerful purposes have been absent.

In thinking about schools in general, as well as our own schools, those in which we live much of our lives or to which we are most committed, we need always to reach back to first things, to guiding purposes, to our richest, most generative conceptions of education and work toward them. These largest purposes need to be fully within our common language. More embedded in our language, more a part of our thought about teaching and learning, our practice should assume some different and more consonant directions.

Two

Deciding What to Teach

In too many school systems teachers are not expected to make significant decisions about what to teach. And the decisions that are open to them often have fairly rigid boundaries. Elaborate curriculum guides with detailed objectives organized around subject fields and extending to the sequence of topics to be taught are not uncommon, leaving little room for the personal interest or invention of teachers *or* students. And in some settings these systems are supported by an array of topical, unit, and semester tests to monitor teacher and student progress through the prescribed curriculum.

Schools that organize in such a directive manner most often believe they are guaranteeing a basic level of learning for all students by ensuring that all teachers are following a standard curriculum. But when followed closely, such efforts tend to place serious limits on the learning possibilities for students. Learning in such schools invariably gets reduced to small pieces of knowledge ordered by a predetermined sequence with considerable stress placed on coverage. In the process the fullest human meanings of teaching and learning are reduced to technologies.

If teaching is to be as rewarding and as intellectually challenging as it needs to be to sustain well those currently in classrooms and also ensure a steady supply of socially committed, intelligent men and women to enter and remain in the field, teachers must make the principal decisions about curriculum as it unfolds in *their own classrooms.* And if learning is to be connected to student intentions and needs, as it should be, the curriculum will require a high level of flexibility, situated in relation to *particular* students.

To argue for a greater teacher voice in matters of curriculum doesn't imply that there aren't *any* general understandings that guide decisions about content, even some that school-systemwide committees of teachers might outline or that state agencies might suggest. Just living in a particular culture gives considerable definition to what happens in classrooms and schools. The importance of understanding and being able to use English language is one specific example. Knowledge about the political system, with preparation for full participation in community life, is another. And few teachers need reminders that they are expected, whatever their academic fields or teaching assignments, to instill a love for reading and writing, an understanding of the power of collective thought and cooperative action, an attitude of caring for the environment, and an active concern for the well-being of others. I will return to many of these issues.

When we see teachers (both elementary and secondary) as decision makers about classroom practices, as curriculum makers in the fullest sense, then deciding what to teach will begin with the large purposes I discussed in the opening chapter. If they are not in front of us, guiding the decisions we make, what we do will likely lack coherence and power.

The tie between deciding what to teach and the question of purposes should, of course, be clear. In describing the Gary, Indiana, schools at the turn of the century, Frederick Wirt, the school superintendent, noted that decisions about *what* to teach would flow naturally from a clear articulation of purposes, what the school is aiming toward (Dewey and Dewey, [1915] 1962, p. 143). This point is made clearly, I believe, in *The Promise,* the statement of purpose and mission that guides the Central Park East Secondary School in New York City:

> At CPESS we make an important promise to every student—one we know we can keep. We promise our students that when they graduate from CPESS, they

will have learned to use their minds—and to use their minds well.

In every class, in every subject, students will learn to ask and to answer these questions:

fundamental questions

1. From whose viewpoint are we seeing or reading or hearing? From what angle or perspective?
2. How do we know what we know? What's the evidence, and how reliable is it?
3. How are things, events or people connected to each other? What is the cause and what the effect? How do they "fit" together?
4. So what? Why does it matter? What does it all mean? Who cares?

We are committed to the idea that a diploma is a meaningful piece of paper, not one that says only that the student has "stuck it out" through high school. A CPESS diploma tells the student—and the world—that the student has not only mastered specific fields of study but is curious and thoughtful, above all, has learned "how to learn" and to use his/her learning to deal with new issues and problems [Central Park East Secondary School, 1988].

To take seriously such a promise—and teachers, students, and administrators at Central Park East do—means a flexible curriculum rooted in large questions, classroom discussions that lend themselves to diverse viewpoints, a literature that addresses issues in challenging ways, and an ongoing consciousness about relationships across disciplinary lines and the boundaries of the school itself. It also gives definition to what students do; for example, their reading is from real text, writing involves a concern for sources *and* personal perspectives, social service is expected, and student decision making is encouraged. Curriculum is an important matter at Central Park East. And by keeping *The Promise* before them, teachers ensure that the curriculum has meaning for themselves and their students.

Decisions about what to teach must also take into account a number of large societal imperatives. Given our pluralism, for example, teachers must ensure that students learn about, and I would hope come to appreciate, the various cultures that exist in our country. And in a world growing increasingly interdependent, they must provide students with knowledge about and understanding of the many nations and cultures we must learn to live with more harmoniously and cooperatively.

Further, every teacher, regardless of field, whether defined narrowly or broadly (chemistry or science, English literature or humanities, history or social studies), is a teacher of communication—reading, writing, speaking, listening, thinking. But to say that every teacher has responsibility for reading and writing does not mean all will expertly understand language development and use—though some will, and they should be viewed as important resources. It does mean, though, being attentive to the reading requirements of the materials used, providing entry points for students who need such assistance to ensure understanding, and making frequent and varied writing assignments that are read carefully and responded to thoughtfully.

It would, of course, be helpful if teachers themselves became more active readers and writers, people who talked often about books and shared their writing with colleagues as well as students. Those who haven't taken part in one of the national or regional writing projects (associated, for example, with the National Writing Project from Berkeley, Teachers and Writers Collaborative, or Bread Loaf) should do so. Teachers might also wish to organize or take part in an ongoing teacher reading group. Surveys describe teachers as *very* limited readers, mostly reading just the local newspapers and an occasional news magazine or teacher journal. But teachers who are not active readers, who don't talk about books and articles from a diverse range of sources, contribute to the literacy limitations of students.

Further, all teachers must keep issues of democracy in the forefront of their teaching practices and the kinds of learning activities they ask students to engage in. Schools have always been described as important centers for citizenship education, but they have tended not to be attentive enough to the values of democracy in their practices.

It is also important when thinking about the content of our teaching, the questions we raise, the experiences we provide, the materials we select to read and reflect upon, that schools are not the *only* learning environments in children and young people's lives. They are exposed to, even bombarded by, television, films, radio, newspapers, magazines, fast food restaurants, and billboards. And they hear conversations in the streets and in their homes.

In relation to many of these visual and auditory sources of information, teachers can help by providing their students with appropriate lenses and tools through which to understand these surroundings more fully, to assist them in separating the substance from the discordant noises and surface images. This means, of course, that they don't close the curriculum to the world that their students listen to and look at every day outside school. It is helpful for teachers to know as much as they can about the neighborhoods their students come from, what they encounter in the streets, what the sounds and smells are, what is watched on television, and what the popular music is.

Television—one entry point into the world of student learning beyond the school—can be seriously examined for its racial content, images of family life and urban communities, violence, coverage of world and national events, bias, subliminal messages, advertising appeals, and language authenticity. Such a focused study of television would, I believe, be useful in helping students become more critical viewers. Other aspects of the popular culture can be similarly explored.

As a principle, it is usually more productive within every area of learning to teach *less* more deeply than to teach *more* as a matter of coverage. And what is taught takes on greater significance if it can be related whenever possible to the lives of the students, if it can be seen as making connections physically, spiritually, morally, and historically. Alfred North Whitehead makes this point clearly in his classic *Aims of Education* ([1929] 1959): "Let the main ideas which are introduced into a child's education be few and important, and let them be thrown into every combination possible. The child should make them his own, and should understand their application here and now in the circumstances of his own life" (p. 14). Most of us understand this point well. What we know and understand most fully and take the most intellectual pleasure from grows out of such a circumstance.

John Dewey provides a useful window into this principle about less rather than more in his description of the thematic work of nine-year-olds in the Dewey School in 1898.

> [By following] a few of the great migrations and ex-plorations that opened up the continents of the world, the children built up an idea of the world as a whole, both racially and geographically. In their imaginary travels, they acquired some knowledge of the place of the earth in the universe and its larger physical forces and of the means that man has used to meet or employ them. They then settled down to the study of a specific people in a specific way and learned how, through the agency of individuals, groups of persons have subdued the untoward elements of their physical environments and have utilized the favorable ones. . . . The need to formulate the meaning of their activities, either in conversation or in an oral or written report, in recipe or rule for procedures, in mathematics or in the lab-oratory, in verse for songs, or in dramatic form for formal plays, arose for the most part out of the actual situation of the classrooms or the imagined ones of the historical times they were reliving [Mayhew and Ed-wards, [1936] 1966, pp. 164–165, 349].

Around this study of worldwide migrations these nine-year-olds spent their *entire year*. The intensity of the learning activities was very high. How different such a curriculum is from that which governs practice in 90 percent of the schools in America today.

I also think, regarding this concern about depth, of May Sarton's account in *I Knew a Phoenix* (1959). She notes that her sedentary adult life may well stem from a school environment in 1920s Cambridge, Massachusetts, where she traveled for days along the dusty roads of Athens, spent months climbing the Himalayas and painting the great landscapes of this world, using up so much of her energy, her whole being, that she had to sit and rest in adulthood. Sarton suggests, of course, considerable depth and intensity in her learning. Wouldn't it be wonderful if all our students had such vivid remembrances of their schooling.

To ensure this greater depth and also to break through the isolation that tends to prevail in schools, schoolwide and classroom themes have been helpful starting points. In Central Park East Secondary School, a multigrade integrated curriculum has been organized around two courses: (1) humanities and (2) math, science, and technology. During the school's first year, teachers chose to focus on "explorers and exploration," a fitting theme offering innumerable possibilities in both areas of study: the development of new ideas, literary forms, scientific discoveries, technological breakthroughs, music, and architecture; and the setting of new styles, new ways of thinking, and new ways of knowing. Subsequent overall themes have been "patterns" and "relationships." "Whose America is it?" was a recent theme for the humanities course. Where a common theme exists, teachers certainly have more to talk about together and students see more possibilities for their learning.

Another New York City school focused one year on traditions. During a particular month, distinctive African masks made by kindergarten children and sixth-graders were displayed in the hallways. Teachers had collaborated on finding resources and sharing books and speakers. And children talked across the grade levels about their learning because they had something in common to talk about. Their learning had clearly been enlarged.

The use of themes contributes naturally to studies in depth, in part because ideas can be easily related across various fields of inquiry. But they need to be thought about carefully in order to take from them the fullest range of their possibilities. Working on a theme with others is a way of expanding it, opening up a large array of activities, identifying books, considering subtopics. I often suggest to teachers that they map themes together. Through these collective efforts, everyone tends to come away surprised at the extensiveness.

Student interest is another critical point of departure; it immediately connects ideas, content, resources, ways of thinking, and the possibilities of diverse media to real questions. Teachers often put off some questions growing from student interests by suggesting "We'll come to that next semester" or "You'll have a chance to study that next year," but there are losses from such responses. And while the pursuit of many different questions at any one time may seem confusing, unsystematic, and possibly chaotic, it is likely so only in appearance, not in substance. Teachers who are willing to be learners along with their students can usually find connecting points among student interests.

I often ask teachers to reflect on their own most deeply developed interests, the areas over which they feel the greatest intellectual control. Too few of these interests have had their origins in the schools or have been primarily sustained in the schools. But most could have been started and sustained there. In considering their own biographies they come to see the classroom possibilities in larger terms.

Along with student interests, teachers, too, have interests that need to play a part in decisions about what is taught. Students should see their teachers as enthusiasts for learning, people with a love for a particular genre of literature, a period of history, a particular medium of expression, some aspect of the arts, plants, animals, architecture, and politics. Subject to some developmental constraints and social understandings that teachers need always to keep in mind, these passions *need* to find expression in classrooms. It is clear that teachers can make more interdisciplinary connections to their intellectual passions than to areas of knowledge they have only limited control over. They typically know about a wider range of resources, have more interesting questions to pose and more directions to pursue.

I am reminded of a principal whose school was seen as an educational lighthouse, full of enthusiastic teachers and learners. Being asked, "How do you select your teachers?" she noted that the selection of new staff is a collective activity among herself, teachers, and parents. Then she added, "We look for a sparkle in the prospective teacher's eye. We try to ascertain what motivates, energizes him or her. And when making final decisions, we seek those who complement the other enthusiasms that exist." Her point was that students need teachers with a diverse range of deeply held interests if their education is to be as full as possible, if their interests are to be pursued in depth. I found her perspective genuinely convincing.

Several years ago I met a sixth-grade teacher who was a classical guitarist and a serious student of Japanese language and literature. His students never heard him play and they knew nothing about his use of Japanese language or his deep knowledge of Japanese literature. After two years, he left teaching, sharing with me how dissatisfying it was. Yet his strongest entry points were left outside his classroom.

Acknowledging the importance of teacher interests, a secondary school in the Midwest chose to organize social studies coursework around the interests, creativity, and special capabilities of its teaching staff. It was an experiment to see where such an effort might go. The twelve teachers were asked to suggest particular courses, seminars, and workshops they would like to organize and teach. They could plan activities to last a day, a week, a month, or a full semester.

As the suggestions were brought together, it quickly became apparent that there was a richness of experience and interest among the teaching staff that had not been fully used before. Several teachers had abiding interests in particular periods of history. Others had high levels of understanding in several areas within the various social studies disciplines that had not been included in previous programs. Several were personally interested in pursuing fresh (for them) investigations of specific questions and thought it would be interesting to invite students to pursue these topics with them as fellow learners. Still others wanted to organize activities that used community resources and community members almost entirely. There was, in fact, such a diversity of interests and richness of experiences among the teachers that over eighty activities were included in the preliminary list of offerings.

To accommodate such a range of offerings, the school organized the eighteen-week semester into four four-week and two one-week blocks. It also provided flexible daily time modules for each activity. Differentiation between seniors and sophomores was eliminated; all activities were open to the full range of students within the high school.

The faculty then had to decide which, if any, of the activities should be required, which should be elective, which would count toward fulfilling various social studies requirements (those defined by the school district and the state), and which might not draw enough students to warrant offering the activity. To ensure the richest social studies program possible, the faculty also had to decide if any activities had been overlooked. They determined that the question of required courses or activities would be dealt with on an individual basis. Each faculty member became an adviser to approximately twenty students and met with them individually to plan their programs for the year. The advisers typically suggested *some* of the activities they thought particular students should take. If they felt a student had an inadequate background in any major area they required that the student participate in a related activity.

Social studies in this school became, over the course of the year, a much richer program. Teachers liked it because they were able to teach those things they really enjoyed teaching. They were able, as a result, to maintain their own intense interests. Teachers also found that it was considerably more enjoyable working with students who had, for the most part, elected to participate in a particular class. Students liked the program because they had a much greater choice of activities to select from and most of them were able to find classes they were really interested in taking. The experiment was successful enough to encourage the social studies staff to continue in this direction.

While it could be argued that what this group of teachers engaged in was too complex and could if not carefully monitored lead to considerable fragmentation, it nonetheless acknowledges what is possible when teachers start with their own interests and not those developed externally.

Deciding what to teach needs also to be considered in relation to concerns about student understanding. When I speak of understanding, I mean knowledge that can be used generatively, that extends thought in new, even unanticipated, ways and provides for students a deeper entry into the world. Such a view can be contrasted with the inert knowledge that fills so many of the schools, that has meaning *only* in schools, and is typically forgotten quickly or at best slightly recalled to accommodate the needs of some "cultural literacy" list.

Implied in such a perspective about understanding is the view that we need always to make choices. Some content is more generative than other content. The more generative it is, the greater the possibility that it will lead to deep understanding. Implied also is the belief that content selection and pedagogy are connected.

An example from the study of history might be helpful, since all discussions of appropriate curricula in schools include that field of inquiry. Even though history is commonly studied in the schools, there is ongoing concern in American society about the lack of historical perspective among adults (former elementary and secondary students), about low levels of active citizenship in communities, limited turnout for local, state, and national elections, continuing conflicts in matters of race and class, and sharp divisions over issues of justice and definitions of national interest, all of which have relationships to the rationale typically given for historical studies in schools.

My point is not to suggest that the burden for redress belongs exclusively to the schools or history-related programs. But since historical studies in schools are designed as a framework for enlarging understandings related to such citizenship concerns, it is reasonable to inquire further into the ways historical studies are thought about, organized, and taught.

As I think about all this, I focus attention on essential questions—those questions that build on interest and background knowledge but go beyond that, making important connections to other areas of learning and other places and events in the world. To be more concrete, the Civil War is commonly studied in American history courses. But what do we most want young people to understand as a result of their studies? The conduct of the war, a popular focus, might be interesting, but it may not be the best entry point for examining such an essential question as slavery and its effects on American society. Studying the Civil War generatively would involve topics, experiences, literature, factual knowledge, inquiry skills, and pedagogical approaches that would bring students closer to an understanding of slavery and its aftermath. It is only through an understanding of slavery that racism, affirmative action, and civil rights legislation, the writings of Langston Hughes, Richard Wright, Alex Haley, and Toni Morrison, and the lives of Booker T. Washington, W. E. B. DuBois, and Martin Luther King, among others, can assume the richest possible meaning for the students.

Such a study could also provide an entry into such struggles as those occurring in Northern Ireland, the Middle East, and parts of Africa. The details, the facts may be important building blocks to understanding, but when they are gone, no longer recalled easily, what is left? It is to this larger arena, to the deeper understandings, that we should turn more of our attention.

Overall, a helpful question is this: What do our students need to understand? This involves an ongoing rethinking of conventional curriculum objectives in light of the cultural values that surround us, and a perspective on the kinds of knowledge that are likely to prove most generative and useful. We might ask: What concepts, topics, facts, and strategies will enable students to deal more constructively with their ongoing lives, not just in a narrow practical sense, but in relation to their need to become literate, informed, sensitive, and active participants in the life of their communities?

A complicating factor is the continued pressure on teachers to engage in all the "new" technologies that emerge. Currently, a hot topic is "critical thinking" or just "thinking." This new imperative is often being packaged around a number of published "thinking skills programs." By and large, they tend to be three- to five-step technologies independent of any particular content. "Thinking skills" has become, in many schools, a separate course, possibly suggesting we don't need to think *all* the time, in *all* courses.

In part this, like other "hot" topics, is clearly related to the simplification that has occurred around the content of curriculum. Too much is posed around either-or formulations. President Truman, for example, is portrayed as deciding to "drop the bomb and end the war" rather than "not dropping the bomb and seeing one million Americans killed." When content is reduced in this manner, as it too often is in our schools, decision making appears easy. Thought, let alone "critical thinking," is hardly necessary. Thinking—meaning reflecting, weighing issues and ideas, examining something from many different angles, through a multiplicity of lenses, working through many options—takes time. But to the school world of "time on task," that kind of thinking doesn't work.

Deciding what to teach demands, then, that teachers examine

such hot topics as "thinking" and be prepared to reject them in their packaged forms. It means, also, rethinking the issue of time, recognizing that speed generally means surface learning, not serious inquiry.

As you likely noted, my entry into the question of what to teach is purposely nonprescriptive and also tied closely to pedagogical concerns. We have too much prescription already, and we have engaged in too little thought about the pedagogical implications associated with curriculum decisions. While the curriculum needs some order, it needn't be as tightly drawn as it has become and it should never leave teachers out of what has to be a central decision-making role.

Three

Engaging the Students

In many respects this chapter is intended as a complement to "Deciding What to Teach." It covers much of the same terrain, grounding itself in the belief that what happens for students—the quality of their learning—is the *real* measure of a school. Even as we tend to acknowledge such an outlook, however, we are not always guided by that understanding. In too many instances it seems that almost everything matters *except* students' learning. The intercom goes on incessantly, classes are short or cut shorter to accommodate something else, fragmentation is accepted as the norm, quiet is more honored than talk, the world is shut out of or made only marginal to the curriculum, mechanisms of control are pervasive and occupy considerable time and attention, and expectations are modest. We need to start again, making the students we work with our *primary* concern.

To focus on students is first to be attentive to who they are— their cultural backgrounds, their strengths, the kinds of questions that motivate them. It is also to become increasingly more conscious of the school's esthetic qualities, materials, programs, pedagogical orientation, organizational structures, staffing patterns, connections to community resources and social service agencies, expectations, and relationships to parents and guardians. How teachers envision their work in terms of these things will, in the end, deter-

mine whether or not children and young people's education is full
of possibilities.

While there are many excellent schools across the country, I
must confess that I have seen over the years, along with schools that
are very poor and acknowledged as such, too many marginal schools
that are often viewed in their communities as "good enough." Many
of these "good enough" schools are calm and orderly, brightly
painted and graffiti free; they move their students through the grades
with little show of difficulty, boast graduation rates of 85 percent or
more, produce each year above-average test scores, and send the majority of their students on to various colleges and universities. But
does that make them truly "good enough" schools?

Some students in these settings are actively challenged intellectually through a range of advanced placement courses and honors programs, but *most* students are not in such courses. They are
in a variety of lower-level basic courses where the expectations are
modest. And when I inquire about those who don't complete their
schooling, or observe in special education or vocational classes, or
examine disciplinary records, I tend to meet a high percentage of
students from poor and minority families. This should cause us
concern.

Because these schools are calm and meet community expectations at levels that don't disturb many people *too* much, few questions are raised about them. By and large, though, they do not begin
from student needs or interests. Teaching in most classes is rooted
in secondhand materials. The unspoken, not always fully conscious
bargain Ted Sizer (1984) noted in his visits to hundreds of high
schools across the country is in place: students and teachers have
agreed in a number of ways not to challenge each other, to get
peacefully through the 6-hour days and 180-day years. The motion
of school goes on, the richness of possibility remains submerged.

On the more positive side, however, I meet few people within
these "good enough" schools who are prepared to say that this is
the best they could do, that they can't imagine a better school. We
should always set our sights on the better school, but that should
not cause us to disparage the good work that often exists in these
"good enough" settings. The goal should be to make that exemplary work the norm.

Engaging the students means taking them seriously, acknowledging that they are trying to understand the world in which they live and that what is studied in school must make connections to that underlying intention. It means being alert to students' questions and deep interests, using them as starting points for the content being examined.

A mother once explained to me her son's fascination with the television programs *Nature* and *Nova* and with books about animals and their habitats. Yet, he didn't like his middle school science program, received poor grades in science, and was discouraged by counselors from taking serious science courses in high school. The gap between his strong science interests and what passed for science in school was substantial. I believe these gaps exist in a number of fields. The task for teachers is to become knowledgeable enough about their students' particular interests to build a substantial part of the curriculum around them.

When teachers know students well—their interests, learning patterns, general stance, the meaning of their gestures, their ways of approaching new materials and fresh ideas, and their outlook on the world—they can more productively engage them on a personal basis, ensuring a deeper entry into learning. Further, and this speaks to the mutuality of teaching, what makes of it a fully human activity, when students know more about their teachers—their particular interests, intellectual passions, knowledge about various topics and resources, commitments, sensitivities, ways of addressing various issues—they are more able to engage them, to pose particular questions, and to seek productive counsel.

For teachers and students to come to know each other well demands settings in which they have opportunities to work with each other over time and in diverse ways. Elementary schools would do well to organize in such a manner that a small group of teachers might work with a relatively small group of students over an extended period, possibly three to five years. Having a single teacher stay with a group of children for at least two years, possibly longer, is also helpful. Restructuring secondary schools around small teams of teachers and students can serve a similar purpose. Communities have to be constructed within schools around the understanding that students and teachers have to be *well known*.

To say, as I have, that students' starting points are critical does not mean, of course, that new and broader interests cannot be cultivated throughout the school experience. The larger the array and diversity of materials, the more varied the approaches to the teaching–learning exchange, the broader the questions raised, the more varied the media, the more experience provided to children and young people in and out of the school, the more opportunities there are for students and teachers to meet individually and in small groups, the greater the potential for fresh interests to develop.

Children interested in butterflies may, for example, be first attracted by their colors or their movements (essentially their esthetic qualities); later, by questions posed, by the interests of others, by closer observation, they become interested in their life cycles, periods of dormancy, and activity. Such interests could go in many directions, even beyond butterflies. But in many classrooms student interests are cut off at an early point because they aren't associated directly with the planned curriculum or they are seen as taking too long to pursue.

The student who asks, for example, about the cost of chickens, or some other commodity, in the middle ages, who wonders whether they had a similar value within a barter system as now, is raising an interesting economic and historical question. It might take weeks of effort to get close to that kind of question but the potential is nonetheless large, even if we don't see it as a central question, generative of an ongoing understanding of the world. Interests, of course, don't always have to end in easily apparent "useful" knowledge.

Attitudes of inquiry should always be encouraged. Learning to use resources, to find answers to personal questions, is always useful. And when students have the opportunity to pursue their individual interests in depth, the greater is the potential for them to interest others along the way. There is considerable power in peer interactions.

To focus so much attention on interests may seem excessive. But we need to tilt the work of the classroom in such a direction. Where we are now is not particularly productive. This doesn't mean that learning is easy or should be seen as easy, that it is not often accompanied by intellectual, physical, and emotional tension. But it ought never to be just plain repetitious and boring. Few individuals reject hard work that is aligned to interest or related to important purposes.

In this vein, using language as the example, John Dewey suggests that schools often disengage students by separating what is taught from student expression. He writes: "When there are no vital interests appealed to in the school, when language is used simply for the repetition of lessons, it is not surprising that one of the chief difficulties of school work has come to be instruction in the mother tongue. Since the language taught is unnatural, not growing out of the real desire to communicate vital impressions and convictions, the freedom of children in its use gradually disappears, until finally the high school teacher has to invent all kinds of devices to assist in getting any spontaneous and full use of speech" (Dewey, [1899] 1956, pp. 55–56).

The point is that we engage our students most productively by placing before them questions that are real and providing the fullest context possible for the content to be discussed. Students need to understand throughout their schooling that mathematics, for example, is *more* than adding, subtracting, multiplying, and dividing unsituated numerals, that science is *more* than chemical formulas and nomenclature, and that history is *more* than dates and male presidents and generals. If we wish to engage students successfully, we need to make each area of study larger than the convention that prevails.

Moreover, it is not helpful to present simplistic either–or constructs, as if only two possibilities can exist. Most of our students know there must be many more, even as they give us the two we want. It is also important to help students to understand more fully the constructivist nature of most knowledge, to see that most topics are surrounded by multiple interpretations.

Part of the simplicity that accompanies what is typically taught in schools has, of course, a political base or a fear of breaking with convention. A personal experience might help here. Politically active students in a high school in which I taught, not too many years after *Sputnik* and in the midst of a worsening of relationships with the Soviet Union, petitioned to the school board for a course in comparative governments and economic systems. They also ap-

pealed to the board to have me assigned to the course. After several
months of debate and considerable pressure from the students, the
board decided that such a course should be offered and that I was
to be the teacher.

The decision produced a bit of a panic at the central curriculum department. The curriculum coordinator and a panel of advisers (which didn't include me) selected the text for the course and
produced what they believed would be a safe outline for what was
considered a "very controversial" course. The title of the text was
Democracy vs. Communism (which seemed to me an intellectually
inappropriate title for a course in comparative governments and
economic systems). Within the early pages was a cartoon of ordinary
Russian people going through a sausage machine, coming out at
the other end as fierce-looking soldiers, marching in precision, with
weapons at an attack position. The text was xenophobic and simplistic. After offering a complaint that it would be disrespectful of
the students if I put this book before them, that serious students
needed to be taken seriously, I was told that the curriculum committee had done what it was supposed to do and the course was now
in my hands. The textbook stayed in a closet until the last week of
the semester, when I passed it out for review. It served to make a
point about fear, about the uses of nationalistic rhetoric and bias,
but it would have taken the heart out of the course if it had been
the text.

Students are also engaged more fully when they know that
teachers care deeply about the world, are moved, for example, by the
loss of life in an air crash, the effects of the drought on families in
the Plains states, the sufferings of children in the Sudan. This point
is also connected to my belief that teachers need to be well known.

Teachers provide children and young people with important
portrayals of their outward caring by being active in community
life, working to keep the streets safe, the libraries open, and the
parks clean. Teachers who are advocates for children and families,
for quality housing for all, for adequate health care for seniors, and
for an end to racial and ethnic discrimination contribute greatly to
young people's understandings of how their communities work and
what it means to care for a community's well-being. While I am

aware that teachers can't engage in all these activities all the time, I trust that my principal point is clear.

In a related vein, I often meet teachers who live different personas, being rigid, low-keyed, nonspontaneous in their classrooms and lively outside school. They are skillful musicians, but their students have never heard them play. They write, yet their students have never read any of their writing. They are birdwatchers, students of urban architecture, collectors of rare books, jazz enthusiasts, peace activists, kayakers, mountain climbers, and wood finishers, but have never brought those avocations to their students. Such separation in what teachers engage in within and outside classrooms needs to be thought about again.

Jonathan Kozol notes, "The concept of professional behavior, as it has been defined . . . is devoid of almost all intensities . . . all that we love in drama, all that we find breathtaking in a film, all that is tragic, comic, intense, extreme, remarkable, is filtered from the teacher's manner. If film and drama were restricted to the range of feelings present in this type of classroom, the theaters would quickly empty and people would pour out into the streets" (Kozol, 1981, p. 12).

Teachers needn't reveal themselves completely; few people do this, even among good friends. But they need to be seen as *real* people who care, have strong beliefs, live fully in the world. The logic of this seems clear enough to most teachers I encounter, yet there remains a legacy that offers a contrary message. Young teachers are often reminded, for example, "not to smile until Christmas," that old code phrase for maintaining one's distance, keeping students off guard, not revealing too much, giving students a little fear from the uncertainties.

Everywhere, it seems, discipline, the need to "maintain control," has come to dominate much of the discourse of teaching. (The fact that schools tend to be too large contributes, I believe, to the obsession over control.) It is almost as if teachers and administrators have come to believe the media reports about violence and disorder in the schools. There may be dangerous schools but the numbers are exceedingly small. The vast majority of schools, whether they are in cities, suburbs, or rural communities, are relatively quiet, mostly pleasant, civil places. If teachers wish to teach, they can, and students can also learn if they choose to.

I believe the limits we need are few, revolving almost exclusively on how individuals treat others in the environment and how they treat each other's work. Most of the negative exchanges in schools between teachers and students stem from too many rules that are rooted mostly in control and not in concern for student learning. Eliot Wigginton is fond of quoting Lao-tzu: "The more laws you have the more thieves there will be" (Wigginton, 1985, p. 257).

Much of the standardization that exists in schools grows out of the belief that control is most easily achieved when everyone in a classroom is working on the same material, when grades are determined by single pieces of work held up to some common standard, when passage from one grade to another has sharp lines of demarcation. But control built on conformity and rigid limits leaves education rather uninteresting. Control can, however, be conceptualized differently—an orderliness in relation to significant learning, materials being available when they are needed, feedback given to students in a timely fashion, groupings that change regularly, time to start and finish projects. When classrooms are lively intellectual settings, discipline is seldom a problem. There is always order.

Order in schools also has a lot to do with the overall climate, whether students and teachers like being there. If they do not, education is difficult. I learn a lot about a school just being in the hallways. When the walls are bare, I wonder if the school as a whole has barren qualities. Charity James, a noted English educator, describes American schools as places "which breed a sense of powerlessness . . . and are designed to institutionalize the human spirit" (James, 1974, p. 27). She was speaking of the school environment. In a school where engaging the students is important, the walls will carry a wide range of educational messages. There will be artwork, announcements about film, art and museum shows, book jackets, newspaper articles, work of students—their writing and painting, posters for theater productions, literary journals, symbols of mathematics and science—photographs of the life of the school, past and present, and symbols of the community in which the school exists.

Observing classroom practices is also revealing. Are the

learning activities varied? Do teachers ask challenging questions? Do they use interesting materials? Do they care for the students? Feel at ease with them? Are the students actively involved?

To engage students constructively, the school day also needs more continuities, not more fragmentation. Work that can truly be valued takes time, sometimes hours and days. It is hardly reasonable to expect a child to complete a fine piece of artwork in ten- or twenty-minute intervals, twice a week, or produce a well-organized, thoughtful description, a poetic or narrative story within ten minutes. Teachers know this but claim that in this current basic skills, testing, "academic" environment, they don't have the time any more for work of that quality. We need to think more about the meaning of quality.

Moreover, and possibly more important, life in classrooms is shaped by the expectations that are held for children. No matter how good a school might appear physically or how many books and computers exist, if teachers don't believe firmly that *all* children can learn and *all* children have important interests, intentions, and strengths that need to be seen as starting points for ongoing learning, they are failing children, their families, and their communities. And when children are seen as failures or deemed not capable of full participation in the best that schools provide, their educational possibilities are stunted. I have been in too many of these schools.

We engage students more fully also when we play down competition and emphasize appreciation for one another. It is uplifting to be in settings where students are used to praising or even clapping for one another when a piece of work is well done, a good story is told, a creative response is given.

Engaging the students constructively means also being concerned about the materials being used in the instructional program. Much that students learn in schools certainly comes from what they read, see, and hear. If their classrooms are full of books, photographs, magazines, newspapers, displays, films, filmstrips, videotapes, audiotapes, and records encompassing a diverse range of topics, ideas, periods of time, genres, and forms, the potential for their learning is large. But few students are in classrooms that bulge with such a diversity and range of materials, guaranteeing them a meager, not very challenging education.

The textbooks, workbooks, and worksheets that dominate classrooms, that have come to guide learning in almost every area of study, provide print but they tend not to present an active, easily envisioned voice; leave little for students or teachers to interpret; don't provoke much imagination; encourage the learning of many parcels of information rather than any significant depth of study; or contribute to school learning assuming a different character than learning that occurs beyond the school. These are large shortcomings. They ensure for many students, especially those whose families are not in a position to provide the enriched experiences and learning materials outside the school environment, an education of limited possibilities.

The pressures to use *all* the basal materials that overwhelm schools have increased. The usual arguments surround standardization, or efficiency, curriculum continuity, and equity (though it needs noting that equity is a recent argument). In large measure, however, the basal materials provide only an illusion of equity. The attempts at standardization and continuity, for example, discourage the appropriate individualization that equity demands. And because everything is so predetermined, student deficits become more prominent than student strengths. This also works against considerations of equity. John Dewey was particularly clear about this point, noting that "there is nothing more blindly obtuse than the convention which supposes that the matter actually contained in textbooks of arithmetic, history, geography . . . is just what will further the educational development of all children" (Dewey, [1934] 1964, p. 4).

In relation to arguments about efficiency—which essentially means ease in teaching and simplicity—Alfred North Whitehead reminds us that if a book "is ever easy to teach from, the book ought to be burned, for it cannot be educational" (Whitehead, [1929] 1959, p. 16). For Whitehead, like Leo Tolstoy and Mark Twain, simplicity should not be seen as a virtue in matters of education. Watching children, and their parents, try to figure out what is to be done with the workbook pages children bring home to complete is only one example. These workbook pages were intended as simplifications for learning. And textbooks, because they try to simplify everything so much, leave out most of what would actually engage the students and help them understand what is being discussed.

When basal materials first became dominant in the schools some one hundred years ago, it was believed that teachers needed them. Otherwise, they wouldn't know how to proceed. This was at a time when teachers had a very limited, mostly precollegiate level, education themselves. Even though teachers are better prepared today in terms of content background, and considerably more educational materials are available for use, these basal materials are *still* pervasive, used in close to 90 percent of all classrooms in America.

Teachers need to understand more fully what the continued dominance of these textbooks, workbooks, and worksheets means. While dependence on these materials works against equity and creativity, and takes time away from more useful, interesting, and engaging materials, it also undermines the professionalism of teachers. It leaves them as intermediaries, managing someone else's conception of education, sequence, and questions. While it is often argued that these materials are developed by "experts," people who understand the various content areas well and know the best entry points for student learning, their audience was "America's students," not the particular children and young people who sit with most teachers I know. Teachers themselves can do better. Importantly, what they produce themselves, what they choose from among the rich possibilities that exist, will have meaning for them and for the students they personally know and care about. Their sense of responsibility will certainly grow, possibly ending the refrain I often hear: "I would never have selected *this* material."

Whitehead criticized educational institutions for fostering "secondhand learning" and focusing on "inert ideas," the ingredients of mediocrity and limited cultural development (Whitehead, [1929] 1959, pp. 3–7). Secondhand learning does not inspire learners, does not cause them to make what they learn personally vital. Textbooks, workbooks, and worksheets are the scaffolds for this secondhand learning.

Rather than textbooks, workbooks, and worksheets, classrooms need to be dominated by *real text*. By that I mean firsthand materials—books with authors and points of view, acknowledged literature, source documents, diaries, newspapers, magazines, and primary accounts of events that push students to react, think, and wonder. A teacher colleague of mine defines real text as material you would give to a friend as a gift. Can you imagine giving a textbook to a friend on a special occasion?

A real text is Walt Whitman's *Leaves of Grass,* not a few paragraphs or a mini-lecture *about* Walt Whitman's poetry. Real text is a videotape of the 1963 civil rights march on Washington and Martin Luther King's "I Have a Dream" speech. Laura Ingalls Wilder's *Little House on the Prairie* stories are real text. So are Charles Darwin's *The Origin of Species,* the Declaration of Independence, the *Federalist* papers, the Coyote stories, the Code of Hammurabi, the Koran and the Bible, *The Iliad* and *The Odyssey.* Photographs of particular Gothic structures, cemetery headstones, land deeds, paintings and sculptures, and diaries are also examples of real text. Students' journal writing, their poetry and imaginative writing and painting, are also real text.

To speak of real text is also to consider various resources designed to extend learning—the reference materials that exist in print, video, and computer libraries, rail, bus, and air schedules, and various maps. The more firsthand these resources are, the closer they are to the world and what people beyond schools use for their learning, the better.

A classroom with a few hundred different books is far preferable to a classroom that has only basal books for all students, regardless of the level or the field. In the video and audio fields, increasingly rich collections of firsthand materials are becoming available, many free of any externally imposed interpretation. The more of these that are available to schools, the better. And the computer, with its access to a wide array of data bases and source materials, also holds considerable potential for enriching classrooms.

Even though I emphasize firsthand accounts, I don't want to suggest that there is *no* room for a secondary account, a synthesis of ideas, an interpretation of an event or a set of ideas. There are times when one or more of these might be useful to particular students, helping them to understand some of the broader, more integrative contours of a topic, providing them additional perspective, giving them another set of questions. But they cannot and ought never to be the center of the educational experience. That these materials continue to dominate the educational experience of students is discouraging.

We need to actively engage the students, making this engagement a conscious effort. I realize that this is easy to say but not so easy to do. But beginning the process is the first step to getting there.

Four

The Community
and the School

The schools we work in exist in neighborhoods and communities. They are often spoken of as the centers of communities, and in some settings, they provide spaces for meetings, a host of educational programs, and entertainment in the form of student plays, musical performances, and sports activities. By and large, though, the interactions between schools and their communities are minimal. They may occupy together physical space, but most often they are worlds apart.

The school as a fortress is not just a metaphor; in many settings it is real. Schools have become institutions with lives of their own, rarely impinging on or having much relationship with the world outside. A school in a lively Puerto Rican neighborhood in Chicago might be, in terms of appearance and curriculum, in what is read and talked about, more like a school in rural Wisconsin.

Children and young people in most schools describe their school learning as something that has very little to do with their lives beyond school. When students speak of the remoteness of school—and they do—they are really talking about the lack of connection between school and the world outside. They are essentially acknowledging what Alfred North Whitehead noted: that most of what is taught in school is not about life "as it is known in the midst of living it."

Students see homelessness and poverty in the streets around them, they know about immigration as they hear so many languages being spoken, they are aware of community violence, drugs, war and the threat of war. That schools don't explore such issues deeply, for the most part even ignoring them, reinforces for students that the schools are about something other than the realities of the world. Further, the content of schools seldom relates to what people in a particular community care deeply about. Schools don't often make the local community architecture or its historical and cultural roots a focus of study. The community's storytellers and craftspeople are not common visitors. The literature that is read is seldom selected because it illuminates the life that students see day in and day out outside the school. This disconnectedness trivializes much of what students learn.

As teachers, we know this intuitively. That's why we make occasional forays into the community—a walk to the park in relation to a science project, going to the local library so every student will get a library card, inviting in a couple of local persons each year to share an experience, having a cultural awareness day related to the special ethnic origins of a dominant community group. Still, such efforts tend to fall in the "enrichment" category, special events surrounding the "real work" of the school—even though teachers and their students often view these efforts as the highlights of the school year. The real work could, of course, be centered a good deal more on the local setting. That could be its starting point. Eliot Wigginton and his Foxfire program firmly make that point. (I recommend to you Wigginton's inspiring 1985 book *Sometimes a Shining Moment.*)

As I think about those in the schools reaching out, making larger connections to the communities that surround them, I come first to parents, the people who initially introduced children to the world and greatly influence children and young people's understandings of that world. While teachers in schools are, to some degree, in touch with their students' parents—notes go home, calls are occasionally made, and brief meetings occur around twice-a-year conferences—they don't as a rule know these parents very well. Their interests, avocations, and skills almost always go unknown and unused in the schools.

If schools are made more accessible to parents, where their presence in the hallways and in classrooms is not so uncommon and where their participation in decision making is significant, the schools can assume a more integrated quality with the world around them. Through their interaction with these additional adults, students can enlarge their interests and come in contact with a far broader range of occupations and lifestyles than would otherwise be the case.

While acknowledging this potential, many teachers have told me that their communities are different, that the adults surrounding their schools, including their children's parents, don't really have much to contribute. My sense is that they really don't know those communities very well, that they are still thinking too narrowly about the possibilities. Most communities are laden with interesting human resources able to offer a great deal to the education of children and young people.

I often think about a young, enthusiastic, well-educated elementary teacher who worked in a small rural community in North Dakota. He had a good understanding of mathematics and psychology, but he knew far less about grains than the local farmers, much less about mechanics than the man at the local garage, less about the riches of the wildlife refuge than the conservation officer, and knew virtually nothing about Japanese customs and cuisine until he met the Japanese woman who had married a local man during his tour of military service in Japan. He enriched his classroom enormously by opening it to these local resources. And he was in a very small town (fewer than two hundred). It takes little imagination to see the human resource potential that must exist in larger communities.

As I reflect on external resources, I am quickly drawn back to Richard Wurman's *Yellow Pages of Learning Resources* (1972). I loved that book when I first read it. It affirmed so much of my outlook about the need to reconceptualize the meaning of a community school. And while I know that many conditions have changed since the book was initially published, the potential for connecting schools and the resources of communities remains large.

Wurman provides a number of entry points for using one's city or town as an extended schoolhouse. He writes: "Education has been thought of as taking place mainly within the confines of the classroom, and school buildings have been regarded as the citadels of knowledge. However, the most extensive facility imaginable for learning is our urban environment" (p. 1). He stresses the need for teachers to become careful observers of their environments, to find in the reality of the world additional learning possibilities. "The city is everywhere around us, and it is ripe with learning resources. . . . But in order to realize the vast learning potential of their resources, we must learn to learn from them . . . learn not to overlook the obvious, . . . hear when we listen, see when we look . . . realize that good questions are better than brilliant answers" (p. 1).

Any place where something special occurs can be a classroom of consequence—churches, medical facilities, museums, libraries, factories, food processing plants, bakeries, garages, supermarkets, airports, ethnic culture centers, and restaurants. And the people who work in these special settings and around the community can be seen as teachers also—the carpenter, the baker, the lawyer down the street, the salesperson in the grocery store.

Excursions out into the community need not involve an entire class. When whole classes are involved, there are typically serious limitations in what is possible, and the necessary planning and control efforts generally work against the activity being fully productive. Teachers usually finish such large, whole-class excursions thinking, "That's the last one!" The local bakery can handle only three to four children at any one time. And the local historical museum might not be willing to take more than twelve. These smaller groups of students can be taken by parents, retired teachers, other senior citizens, and college students. This in itself offers fresh possibilities.

The course I taught most recently in a secondary school, entitled "Growing Up in Grand Forks," drew heavily on Wurman's understandings of the potential of a community serving as a larger schoolhouse, providing much of the content for an intensive education. Its primary purpose, along with enlarging writing and inquiry skills and understandings of how historians and sociologists go about their work, was to enlarge students' consciousness about their own community and their place in it. When we began, few students (they were juniors and seniors) could describe the community in much detail. They hadn't observed carefully the special Romanesque architecture of the downtown buildings or taken note of the community's statues or their origins. Most had never been inside the federal courthouse, the city hall, the Jewish synagogue, the state mill, the downtown art gallery, or the university museum of art. They couldn't identify most of the trees and knew little about city government, tax structures, or the city's development plan. Issues that people cared about—water purity, flood control, recreational uses of the river and its banks, low-income housing policies, the deterioration of the downtown, economic stagnation and tax rates—were not part of their concerns. Few had ever gone to a public hearing about any community issue. Though many were eighteen, they hadn't really thought much about voting. They knew they could, but most told me they didn't really know anything about the issues.

I believe we owe it to our young people to ensure that they are deeply involved *with* their communities, that they leave us eager to take an active part in the political and cultural systems that surround them. Enlarging our vision of the school is vital.

A particular concern with secondary schools is students who work. Close to 70 percent of secondary school students are employed, principally in the burgeoning fast-food industry. Rather than viewing this work as positive, contributing to student responsibility and a sense of usefulness, those in schools speak of it primarily as lessening student commitments to the school's academic and extracurricular programs and fostering what they believe to be an unhealthy materialism (Perrone and others, 1981). Once again it is as if the work of the school and the larger world must be in conflict, that there aren't connecting points of consequence that actually affect the students and their learning.

While I acknowledge that students who work over twenty hours a week (and this encompasses almost half of student workers) tend to suffer academically within the current structure of schools (time bound, restrictive in terms of the number of courses a student must take each semester, and curricularly insular), the work of students needs to be thought about more constructively (as does the structure of schools). Students, for example, speak of what they do in their work as "being useful," "being independent" and "responsible." They also tend to enjoy their work. And employers see them as reliable and competent (Perrone and others, 1981). Are such perspectives to be negated? Is there no way to use such awareness?

I often ask teachers why they don't have students maintain journals of their work experience; why they don't make these work experiences the focus of study in courses in health, nutrition, science, economics, mathematics, government, history, and literature; why they don't engage more directly the materialist culture that is so potent a force in American society and contributes heavily to student employment. Can't the world that these students have entered into so fully be connected to the ongoing and important work of the schools?

Those in the schools talk a great deal about preparing their students for social and civic responsibility, but the opportunities to gain experience in these directions are limited, if they exist at all. It is possible for students to complete their schooling and never be involved deeply, in or outside the school, in any service-oriented activity such as tutoring younger children or classmates, working with the elderly, constructing or maintaining a playground, monitoring a public hearing, completing a community survey, or teaching at a Boys' Club or YWCA. The lack of connections is large. Teaching for social responsibility and active citizenship is in most settings merely rhetoric.

But children from their very early years have a disposition toward outwardness, a need to learn about the world and participate actively in its ongoing life. They have a natural desire to engage others, to be helpful. And if nurtured in the home and in the schools, such a disposition can develop into a fuller form of social and civic responsibility. Some of the wonderful remembrances of teens I have talked with are of particular trees they planted as children. The trees that now bring so much pleasure to their communities stand as visible reminders of their earlier service.

The isolation in students' lives between what they do in and outside school is being addressed in many schools as they become centers for community service. Increasing numbers of schools, in fact, have made service a requirement, while others have made it an integral part of their curriculum. All schools, though, need to build a service ethic.

Central Park East Secondary School, in New York City, has a schoolwide service program that involves all its students *during* the school day. Approximately one-eighth of the students are involved in a service activity each morning and afternoon, Monday through Thursday. Their placements include such settings as the Museum of the City of New York, the Studio Museum of Harlem, Mount Sinai Medical Center, the Association to Benefit Children, the 92nd Street YMHA, the Jewish Guild for the Blind, the Union Settlement House, the Community Planning Board, the Center for Collaborative Education, Head Start programs, and local elementary schools. Efforts are made to integrate the experience students are having in their service placements with their ongoing coursework. And there are many places for connection in a setting where every student is involved and teachers play an active advisory role. Central Park East is an exceptional school in regard to service, but it shouldn't be. Every school could do what Central Park East does if it chose to.

Here I have concentrated on service beyond the school, because the larger, out-of-school community has been my focus. But service can be directed back to the school, aimed at building the community of the school. A social and civic responsibility orientation can certainly be fostered within the school as efforts are made to build the community, to develop more fully its democratic character.

My concern in this chapter is about enlarging the possibilities for students to construct a more productive community-oriented life and helping them to see their learning in more than school terms. That calls for connecting the school and the world beyond the school more directly, blurring wherever possible the lines that separate them.

Five

Valuing Differences

To teach in the schools today, it is necessary to be particularly attentive to differences, to acknowledge the handicapped and non-handicapped, English speaking and non-English speaking, and members of most of the world's racial, ethnic, and religious groups. Our schools have never been as universal nor our population so varied.

While we have long been a nation of immigrants, the principal flow for most of our history was European. But in the past twenty-five years the United States has become the home of several millions of people from the Philippines, Vietnam, Cambodia, Laos, Korea, China, Central America, and the diverse island nations of the Caribbean. The population influx from Mexico has reached unprecedented levels. Our Native American population, while not yet at its nineteenth-century levels, has enlarged considerably, along with our longstanding black population, with roots in America as deep as the dominant white population.

In twenty-three of our largest twenty-five school districts the majority of students come from minority populations; thirty percent of *all* children in the public schools are minority. And a significant percentage of students who come to the schools each day have a first language other than English. (The estimates run as high as 4.5 million, at least 10 percent of those in the schools.) While

45

Spanish is the largest first language for non-English speakers, thirty to forty other languages are relatively common (Council of Great City Schools, 1986).

Beyond all that (and I haven't touched on the totality of the conditions that influence our children's attitudes, dispositions, beliefs, and world views), differences are basic to all human existence. It is out of difference that individuals gain a sense of personal identity, become persons in their own right.

Even though differences are great, common goals, common hopes can still exist. Forms of unity are possible. But unity should not mean cultural submergence, any loss of personal or group identity. Philosopher Harry Broudy offers a perspective: "The heart, liver and brain differ from each other but, by their difference, strengthen the unity of the organism. . . . In art, one theory holds that the test of success is the unification of variety" (Broudy, 1988, p. 226). Martin Luther King in his last written article also shared an important understanding of our need to think in terms of a healthy interrelated mosaic. "Once again we must reaffirm our belief in building a democratic society, in which blacks and whites can live together as brothers, where we will all come to see that integration is not a problem but an opportunity to participate in the beauty of diversity" (King, 1968, p. 183).

Forging a unity among such a large diversity of race, language, religion, ethnicity, and lifestyle is the challenge of our schools and our society. It demands that we face up more fully to the cultural pluralism that exists, that we finally and consciously embrace it. We have been a culturally pluralistic nation for most of our existence. But we have tended to want a single model for defining the good. Over the years the ideal has been described in terms of an Anglo-American middle-class society—essentially involving light-skinned English-speaking people who are competitive and acquisitional. American school readers from McGuffy to *Dick and Jane* placed such an ideal before tens of millions of children over close to ninety years of our educational history.

Most differences of race and cultural background have been seen as problems to be overcome through assimilation to "the more ideal state." For the American Indian, the Carlisle School in the latter years of the nineteenth century was the epitome of official public policy. The founder of Carlisle, Richard Pratt, thought the only way to solve the "Indian problem" was to make sure Indian children *lost* all connections to their culture. He noted in his memoirs: "I believe in immersing the Indians in our civilization and when we get them under holding them there until they are thoroughly soaked" (Pratt, 1964, p. 335). *The Red Man,* the journal of Carlisle, made Pratt's view clear. It always included "before and after" photographs. The "before" pictures were of young men with blankets over their shoulders and long braided hair. The "after" pictures had them in black tuxedos and top hats with an obvious military haircut. Carlisle was, of course, only one of the many nineteenth- and twentieth-century boarding schools aimed at this kind of deculturalization.

For the new immigrants of the late nineteenth and early twentieth centuries, there was talk of a melting pot, some merging of the best features of all backgrounds into a single crucible from which a new culture might emerge. But assimilation was the dominant policy and hope. Schools tended to be rather tenacious in keeping children's first languages out of the schools, and immigrant ways were held up as backward and inferior. Children learned shame, not pride in their cultural roots.

For blacks, their skin color made the assimilationist's task more difficult. Segregation was legally sanctioned and a language of inferiority was used to justify negative race-oriented policies. In the schools, as desegregation became official public policy, one implicit though seldom articulated formulation was the belief that when black children were put with white children, they would become more like white children. Assimilationist thought was still an important guiding force. The long-standing racism that has accompanied white–black relationships remained close by in those early desegregation years, and it remains with us still.

Differences are in front of us as never before. How we respond is particularly important. Shall we see differences as a problem to be overcome or a matter of celebration, a constructive challenge to our structures, pedagogies, and curriculum? For the most part we aren't in a very good place with regard to this. We don't speak overtly the language of assimilation or of racism, but nonetheless we have terms that implicitly suggest both—"culturally impoverished," "disadvantaged," "language deficient," "passive," "those children."

We have struggled in the schools to engage issues of race and cultural differences constructively, but we haven't yet learned how to speak about such matters, embedded as they are with guilt, shame, confusion, superiority, and inferiority. Even as we tend to acknowledge that race and issues of difference need to be central to the curriculum, that curriculum is virtually absent. Our challenge is to make the school a safe setting to engage in conversation and serious inquiry about race and cultural difference. If the schools aren't such a place, where else will these conversations occur constructively?

One of the most common ways to "attend" to differences in the schools currently is through a variety of separation mechanisms—special education, gifted and talented programs, bilingual and bicultural programs, and a variety of "ability" grouping efforts within basic courses and academic areas. Such tracking/separation efforts have reached unprecedented levels. And though generally couched in terms of equity, ensuring personalized attention to students in relation to their needs, it is seldom as benign as that.

While this form of separation has negative effects for *most* children and young people, it works to the greatest disadvantage of blacks, Hispanics, and limited English speakers who tend to be overplaced in special education and lower tracks where their educational possibilities are stunted enormously. Heterogeneity, what I would call the only real source for equity, a structure in which differences can be made the basis for a powerful education for *all* students, is viewed in the majority of our schools as unworkable. Yet, it is seldom tried.

Besides separation, which has mostly negative consequences, the schools have also begun, at least rhetorically, to embrace multicultural education as a way of attending to differences. In theory, the multicultural education movement addresses differences constructively, supporting diverse students and their families, giving attention to cultural richness, acknowledging that there are many perspectives on the world, its history, art forms, language, and literature, and encouraging individuals to be whatever they are with dignity and freedom. And there is much in the multicultural literature to suggest that the schools need to reconstruct themselves to meet the diversity of their students. But multiculturalism has meant in the majority of schools an "Indian Day," a "Puerto Rican Day," possibly a "Black History Week." In few schools has multiculturalism brought the reconstruction of curriculum, pedagogical practices, materials, teacher–student and school–community relationships that such a formulation suggests.

One serious detriment to multiculturalism is the limited number of teachers of color, of different cultural traditions, in our schools. We need to be much more aware of the significant crisis that exists around the recruitment and retention of black, Hispanic, Asian, Native American, and bilingual teachers.

The peak year for minority teachers, for example, was 1972 when approximately 12 percent of all teachers came from these backgrounds. (And few would argue that this level was satisfactory.) At that time, black, Hispanic, Asian, and Native American enrollment in the schools was 20 percent of the total. Today, approximately 9 percent of all teachers are minority and the minority enrollment in the schools is over 30 percent (American Association of Colleges of Teacher Education, 1988). Current projections, based on a variety of teacher education and teacher retirement data, suggest that this important teacher population could decline further through the 1990s, even as black, Hispanic, Asian, and Native American enrollments continue to rise. This is *very* troubling.

Alongside this racial dimension is a language dimension as well. There is an enormous shortage of bilingual teachers able to meet constructively the growing numbers of non–English-speaking children in the schools. "English only" is *not* an acceptable answer. Support for diverse languages is absolutely essential. Otherwise, we place severe limits on more generations of young men and women.

These concerns about minority and bilingual teachers have received too little attention in this era of educational reform. They suggest a public-policy need of *immense* proportions at both the federal and state levels in terms of grant programs and support for those institutions that have historically attracted significant numbers of minority and second-language applicants into teaching. Fresh efforts to make teaching a more attractive field in local schools that serve large numbers of students from these particular communities are also necessary.

Long conscious personally of differences, seeing them as something teachers especially need to understand and certainly work with optimistically, I found my memory tapped in a *different* manner recently. The preservice students I was working with asked several times, "Are we being prepared to teach in an urban or suburban setting?" I want to share some of the thinking this question sparked for me. My hope is that it will also cause you to think further about your experience.

Leaving aside the fact that differences exist within every setting, whether urban or suburban, there was for many of these students a belief that each and every setting demands a *special* preparation—not just in relation to the practical experience component but in what is read and thought about, in pedagogical and philosophical directions, in curriculum formulations. It was almost as if difference should be a call for separation.

I thought about our class readings and asked myself, Is Maxine Greene's "Wide-Awakeness and the Moral Life" (Greene, 1978) (an essay that asks teachers to be more observant of their surroundings and to speak out about moral concerns) related particularly to urban or suburban education? Is there a *particular* audience for Alfred North Whitehead's *Aims of Education* ([1929] 1959)? Are his ideas about learning rhythms applicable to African-Americans and Hispanics and Asians? And can those who think of themselves as preparing to be urban teachers really pay attention to John Dewey, who speaks of community studies and the need for a slower pace, at a time when many urban students are not in powerful literacy environments, their communities are unsafe, and time is a luxury they don't have?

In general, I tended to respond that teaching, wherever it occurs, by being first and foremost an intellectual and moral endeavor, *is* about differences—being conscious of them, attending to them, and, where they apply to children, their parents, and their cultural communities, valuing them. And further, that such a view doesn't imply *one* distinct education for blacks and Hispanics and another for whites; one for those who live in the cities and another for those who live in the country. We know a lot about how the corollary of that particular formulation has been translated. It is filled with differential expectations and unconscionable inequities.

Often when confronted with unexpected questions, I reflect on my own experience. In this case I was prompted to think about my later childhood, early adolescent years, a period framed historically by World War II and the beginnings of the Korean War. There were in those years—as there continue to be now—many contradictory social-cultural threads in relation to America's diverse peoples. Intercultural education, an invention of the 1920s, was in my own school years an important part of the curriculum. While my historical studies suggest that this movement was quite powerful intellectually in the 1920s, by the 1940s, it had become cliché ridden and full of pieties. Why does that so often happen as ideas pass into general use?

The message in simplified terms was that people are people, that differences are very thin, never large, and similarities are overwhelming. (That is often the message that now flows with multicultural education.) A complementary message, though seldom articulated by the teachers, was that failure could almost always be explained by individual laziness and slovenliness. Inherent in the focus on similarities was also a message that differences were negative. That might not have been the intent but how could it have been otherwise? While I wasn't particularly conscious of this at the time, I have over the years come to understand more fully that a preoccupation with similarities, seeing them as positive and differences as negative, tends also to strike hard at areas beyond cultural pluralism. Children viewed as too active, for example, are often removed from regular classrooms or placed on sedatives to reduce their activity levels. Much of the standardization in schools relates to this preoccupation as well—everyone reading the same books and kept at the same pace alongside the same narrow frame of acceptable behavior.

There wasn't much intentional notice given to differences in the elementary school I attended. Though there were fairly large numbers of blacks and Hispanics in the school, most weren't attended to very well. I don't remember *any* who served on the safety patrol, the really prestige enterprise, or were involved in any of the school-related clubs or sports teams. Nonetheless, the message of the classroom was that everyone was basically the same. And later in the secondary school, I don't recall anyone asking why there weren't any Hispanic or black students in senior math, or physics, or advanced composition, or why they seemed so invisible when they were at least 25 percent of the student body. We read nothing in our schoolwork written by a black, Latin American, or Asian—and this wasn't seen as unusual.

As my high school years began to close, the language of interculturalism began to fade away, receiving increasingly less attention. I suspect this happened because the public contradictions couldn't be dealt with.

In more recent years I have found my way back into the diversity of urban settings where traditional minority populations, along with record numbers of new immigrants, are large and visible. The differences stand out, and yet there is so much denial of the difference. One educational framework is still supposed to work for all, one textbook series, one assessment format, one definition of success. And there is continual confusion about how to think about, let alone address language and culture issues.

A ninth-grade Cambodian student, Noy Chou, in suburban Boston, offers well, I believe, a contemporary view of some of these issues (Denzer and Wheelock, 1990, p. 84). Her poem, which I present in part, depicts vividly, poignantly what it feels like to be an outsider in a school that fails to use the full resources of biculturalism for enriching the education of all students.

> What is it like to be an outsider?
> What is it like to sit in the class where everyone has
>   blond hair and you have black hair?
> What is it like when the teacher says, "Whoever wasn't
>   born here raise your hand."
> And you are the only one.
> Then, when you raise your hand, everybody looks at
>   you and makes fun of you.
> You have to live in somebody else's country to
>   understand. . . .
> What is it like when you are an opposite?
> When you wear the clothes of your country and they

think you are crazy to wear these clothes and you
think they are pretty.
You have to live in somebody else's country to understand. . . .
What is it like when you try to talk and you don't
pronounce the words right?
They don't understand you.
They laugh at you but you don't know that they are
laughing at you, and you start to laugh with them.
They say, "Are you crazy, laughing at yourself? Go
get lost, girl."
You have to live in somebody else's country without
a language to understand.
What is it like when you walk in the street and every-
body turns around to look at you and you don't
know that they are looking at you?
Then, when you find out, you want to hide your face
but you don't know where to hide because they are
everywhere.
You have to live in somebody else's country to
understand.

But it is not "somebody else's country," it is Noy Chou's
country as it is mine and yours. We are being confronted as never
before in our schools with differences that need to be acknowledged
as well as made integral to the unity that exists among human be-
ings. People must be seen as individuals as well as members of
groups. How might a focus on differences translate into equally
powerful understandings for all individuals regardless of their backgrounds? Can a person be an Italian-American, Korean-American,
African-American, or Appalachian American, having learned fully
what that means, and still be educated sufficiently to be an active,
powerful participant in the fullness of American society? Assuming,
of course, that the answer is positive, what does it imply for
curriculum?

In many schools, two-way bilingual programs exist, settings
in which there are equal numbers of non–English-speaking and
English-speaking students. Some children are there principally to

learn more English as their native language and culture are provided respect, and others are there to learn, for example, Spanish.

In a school that honors difference, there will be greater flexibility regarding school schedules and curriculum materials and subject matter. Themes will be consciously multicultural. The diverse lifestyles and cultures of children and their communities can, in fact, form a good share of the curriculum. And families will be taken more seriously as full partners. Schools will become untracked. And the tests that have played such a long and powerful role in contributing to separation will assume increasingly smaller roles.

Donald Thomas in *The Schools Next Time* (1973) suggests that "attainment of equal educational opportunity depends upon recognition of diversity first, in all its aspects and then deliberate acting to sustain that diversity with honor. The importance of being equal is that it may be the only way America and each of us can survive" (p. 87). I believe he is right.

My purpose in this chapter is to raise issues of difference to a fuller consciousness, not to cover the arena of multiculturism or racism. Think about differences in your own settings. Where are you with *your* understandings? How can you begin to acknowledge differences constructively?

Six

Evaluating and
Grading Student Performance

In schools, evaluation means mostly grading, a process whereby student work and action are generally reduced to a letter (*A, B, C, D, F*), a number (1-10 or 1-100), or a mark (+, √ or -). And it is seldom accompanied by much teacher or student enthusiasm. Few aspects of teaching, in fact, create so much anxiety.

Though I always argue for *evaluation* as a means of informing, guiding, and supporting the growth of students, as well as meeting some of the legitimate public concerns for accountability (which I address in the next chapter), classroom *grading* does provide difficulties. By and large, it calls upon teachers to rank-order student work and activity, in the process inviting comparisons between and among students. Few of us entered teaching for such a purpose. And I seldom meet teachers who *really* believe it is essential, a practice that stands between learning and not learning, standards and no standards (arguments often used in favor of grades that differentiate performance).

Even as the process is discomforting, those who wield the most authority in the matter (and tradition alone accounts for much of the authority) insist that parents *want* these comparisons. But when parents express ambivalence, which they often do, or pose challenging questions about fairness, which they would likely do more often if the entire process wasn't so tension filled, the argu-

ment shifts to the need to satisfy the demands of colleges or employers. The entire discussion about grading, as well as about evaluation
more broadly, is really quite moribund. It needs again more serious
and sustained deliberation among teachers and parents and between
schools and colleges.

As a way of beginning such deliberations at the school level,
I often ask teachers and prospective teachers (as well as parents) to
reflect carefully on their own experiences with grading and evaluation when they were students. As you are aware by now, I believe
our personal biographies are rich and need to be reflected upon
more often in relation to our ongoing work as teachers. Some of the
following questions serve as guides to the first part of this reflection:
Have you ever felt that an evaluation—of a paper, a presentation,
a test or examination—was unfair? Caused you to be upset? Les-
sened your interest in a subject or course? *What made it so?*

Usually, as you might expect, there is a flood of emotion-
filled remembrances. As students, most of us had some difficulties
with the grading process. What we likely didn't understand at the
time is that teachers also had problems with it all.

One story that came up at a recent discussion began with a
substitute teacher in a third-grade classroom asking the children to
write a "get well, thinking about you" note to their regular teacher,
who was in the hospital. The person telling the story recounted that
the joy of writing the note and his genuine concern for the teacher
were torn asunder when he got his note back a week later with a
number of red marks and a C- grade. While those who heard the
story laughed heartily, the storyteller could *still* feel the anger and
the hurt.

This first reflection activity is followed by a second, posing
such questions as: When did you feel that an evaluation activity was
helpful to you as a student? Assisted you in going forward more
constructively? Enlarged your understanding? *What made it so?*

There are always fewer responses to the second set of questions, which is in itself revealing. The more positive responses stimulated by this inquiry are typically connected to activities the
recounters as students had a large part in selecting and in which
the teachers took an active interest. In a large share of these cases
the narrative responses and personal comments of teachers assumed

far more meaning than the grades. In fact, the tellers of these stories often couldn't remember the actual grades they received.

Occasionally, I have also inquired about experiences with ungraded or less conventional systems, where teachers and students received only narrative comments and a credit received (*CR*) notation, or something similar. Interestingly, these nonconventional systems are often remembered as having encouraged serious learning or "my best work." My personal experience with such systems leads me to believe that a more focused attention to learning tends to result. Not receiving an *A* or *B* or *C* has caused very few people I have discussed this with to *stop* intensive study or feel that they didn't have to take a piece of writing seriously or not do as much research on a topic as they might otherwise have done.

Reflecting on these grading and evaluation experiences from our personal biographies can help us think more about our own approaches to grading, pointing out ways to attend more fully to *constructive* directions. In addition, it should also remind us of the complexities, causing us to consider again such questions as: Must grading include the comparison of students? Is a class rank essential? Is a failing grade *ever* necessary? Would all learning stop if grades weren't given? If there were no failing grade, would standards actually decline?

Assigning a grade to the work of students—deciding that a particular piece of work has a value of *A* or *C* or *F*, that the cumulative value of an individual's involvement over six to eight weeks or a semester should be equated to a *B* or a *D*, or whatever—is never easy, whether in a teacher's first or twenty-fifth year of teaching. Those who have told me that they don't have any real trouble with grading, that it's "easy enough," tend to cause me worry.

However we rationalize the grades we give, they are never *just* about the speech the student gave or the paper that was written; they are about the student. The process can get tied up quickly into issues of self-worth. I think we all know this when we push hard around the edges of grading practices. It is important for us to hold this understanding fully within our consciousness.

A historical review of grading schemes is a good indicator that the entire construct is complex, not necessarily connected to any convincing theoretical or practice-oriented formulation. Following the record in the Philadelphia schools over the past eighty years might be instructive.

1913–1922	Students were graded on a 1–10 scale for their work, supposedly providing for greater differentiation.
1922–1934	Grading reverted to a pre-1913 pattern of *A, B, C, D,* and *E.*
1934–1940	A three-point scale was used: +, -, and checkmark.
1940–1948	All grades became Pass (*P*) or Fail (*F*).
1948–1954	A four-point scale (*A, B, C,* and *D*) was used. Failure was eliminated.
1954–present	The *F* grade was added to the four-point scale.

Practices at Yale from 1960 to 1975 are also instructive. The institution went from a six-point scale of *A, B, C, D, E,* and *F,* to Pass (*P*) and Fail (*F*) in 1963, followed in 1968 by Honors (*H*), High Pass (*HP*), Pass (*P*), and Fail (*F*), but without any computed grade-point average. In 1971, a four-point scale of *A, B, C,* and *D* was introduced, and in 1975, the *F* grade was brought back.

I have, over the years, also seen many other variations— Credit (*C*) and No Credit (*NC*), Satisfactory (*S*) and Unsatisfactory (*U*), or Needs Improvement (*NI*), percentages that are then given letter-grade equivalencies but are retained as numerals for purposes of class standing, and pluses and minuses added to *A, B, C* grades, as well as narrative accounts exclusively or some kind of marking augmented by narratives. The sheer volume of adaptations, along with the movements back and forth, must tell us the ground is soft.

My own preference in terms of what I believe enhances learning has been the narrative with a credit received (*CR*) as the reporting notation for the end of a cycle (a marking period or semester). The most common is still the five-point *A, B, C, D, F* scale, but some schools are trying to get rid of *all* grades and marks that invite comparisons. We are moving into a more experimental period again.

For those pursuing alternative directions, my advice is that you talk a good deal about what you expect to result from the change; that you understand clearly that the purpose of moving away from more conventional systems is not to engage in *less* serious evaluation but in *more* serious evaluation; that you be willing to invest the time that this more serious evaluation will take, and it will most likely take a good deal more time; that you provide ongoing information to parents and students, ensuring that they understand that the process is intended to enlarge student learning and create conditions for more interesting and challenging teaching; and finally, that you create a mechanism to monitor the process in relation to your expectations. One last point: you need to know that changing the evaluation system implies rethinking also the instructional program, pedagogical approaches, teacher–student relationships, and teacher–parent relationships.

The most common fresh form for classroom evaluation is to tie student work to inquiry *or* performance objectives supported by the maintenance of portfolios or exhibits of student learning. Such systems are maintained by a heavy investment in teacher-prepared narratives and frequent conferences with students, plus regularly scheduled conferences involving the students and their parents.

Recognizing that grading practices are related to concerns about college entrance, the Coalition of Essential Schools, which is encouraging the development of exhibits, is also beginning conversations with colleges and universities about alternative ways of reviewing students' high school academic records. Colleges have been positive about this, understanding that the schools can provide rich information to support their students' applications. (Those interested in an earlier history of this kind might want to read Wilfred Aiken's *The Story of the Eight Year Study* [1942], the report of a 1930s study.)

I can't offer a foolproof method of making the evaluation of students' work easy or altogether comfortable in the environment that prevails in most schools, even though I could probably provide an authoritative-looking text. As comforting as such a text might be, however, it would not be genuine enough. I know that, as do you. But I do wish to offer some directions that might either confirm what you already do or suggest other ways to proceed or think about the issues.

As is the case in all aspects of teaching, it is important when considering evaluation to begin with *first things*. Evaluation is first about student growth. Whether it is connected to quizzes, tests, papers, or student observations of particular phenomena, evaluation needs to be thought about in relation to large purposes. For example, if the central purpose of a particular unit is an understanding of slavery, how does *this* student paper (or project) you are evaluating contribute? What do you expect to learn that will assist you in ensuring that students come to deeper understandings of slavery? When the purposes for what students are asked to do are set clearly in mind, evaluation is always more manageable, even if still complex.

Within the constraints of having in most settings too many students, and in the case of secondary teachers meeting the students each day in relatively short periods (forty-two to fifty minutes on average), it is important to find as many *different* ways as possible for students to share with you their understandings of the content under study. This is a constructive way of ensuring that students know you have high expectations for them and that your *primary* interest is in helping them be successful learners.

In far too many classrooms, there is only *one* way—*the* paper on a prescribed topic prepared according to a particular format, *the* speech, *the* text. The more students have options, some control over the questions and possibilities, the better. When students are successful, the teacher's job is easier and more satisfying.

This question of options is related also to the issue of motivation. One thing we do know about children and young people is that they are interested in competence. They are never unmotivated to be successful. To ensure success, students need to have some choices in what they do, opportunities to work as much as possible from their strengths. Closely related is the need for students to have opportunities to appraise their own growth as learners, set against their teachers' largest hopes as well as their own. Self-evaluation is an important ingredient of becoming an independent learner. If students who are asked, "How are you doing in social studies?" respond by saying, "I don't know, you'll have to ask my teacher," the evaluation process isn't working very well. It is stuck in the conventions at their worst—and in most settings that is about where we are.

With regard to written papers, there is often a good deal of confusion over the role of mechanics, to the point where the content of what students present is undervalued. Because the mechanics always stand out in such high relief—it's hard to overlook misspellings, lack of appropriate punctuation, and nonexistent verbs—they dominate most evaluations. It might be helpful to separate content, logic of argument, and mechanics, evaluating them (commenting on them) independently. Students in many settings are now confused about what is being responded to and what they need to work on.

Further, most written work should carry the proviso that it can be rewritten at any time and reevaluated in some form. This is another message that our ongoing interest is in students' *best* work. Such a policy may also help students enlarge their own understandings of appropriate standards for written work, enhancing self-evaluation.

One last point with regard to written work: If we expect students to take writing seriously, they have to know that their work is read carefully and thoughtfully. "Good work!" is hardly an indication that their writing has been read with care and attention. But that, along with a grade and circles around mechanical mistakes, is what students typically see. It isn't good enough. Teachers need to respond to the particular ideas, the metaphors, the force of the arguments, the special understandings, the clarity of expression, as well as offer ideas for extension of thought, alternative directions, and new sources for review.

Examinations are often a part of the environment of schools. But they tend to be given within frameworks that are different from the normal classroom process. Everything has to be finished in a prescribed time. Speed is encouraged. There is no talking and no reference materials are permitted. While I don't see such efforts as the *best* means of helping students pull ideas together, or demonstrate their learning, examinations may, *on occasion*, serve productive purposes.

Many teachers use take-home examinations as a way of providing students time to bring ideas together, to relate various aspects of the context under study, and also to do their best work. This process makes the exam more like other instructional activities, not something that stands so far apart. Others permit reference materials during an in-class exam period. Essentially, they are stressing the importance of the *use* of information, not its *memorization*. (Why do we place so much stress on memorization of knowledge to be given back under stressful circumstances?)

I learned a good lesson about exams very early in my teaching career from a sixteen-year-old. He had not really done well on the first exam, which consisted of four essay questions. In my conference with him (I established a conference with every student who hadn't done well), the student wanted to assure me that he had really learned a great deal about the Greeks but I had asked him *all* the wrong questions. I asked him to state four questions that he judged to be important that he could have dealt with better and then to share with me how he would have responded to them—and he did! He knew and understood more about the subject than his performance on *my* exam would suggest. After that, I often asked students to write questions they believed went to the heart of our studies and then to answer a sample of them. And I made clear to them that the overall quality of their questions was as important as their answers.

Teachers in a number of settings have entered into contractual arrangements with students, essentially establishing what has to be done for a *C*, a *B*, an *A*. Such a process provides students with choices, but it may, based on my observations, also work against students doing their best work or taking enough of the responsibility for their learning. In my discussions with teachers who use such a process, what I hear most is that "it reduces much of the debate about 'why did I only get a *C*?'" Getting rid of such debate is salutary but it leaves other questions unanswered.

One last point: evaluation is not something that occurs only on Friday when a test is given, at the end of four weeks when a big paper is due or a speech is to be made. It has to be more continuous. Teachers need to be closer to student efforts as they are proceeding. Remember, our task is not to see how our students do on one particular day but to know how it's going along the way, ensuring that they will be successful whenever the big day comes. We should never be surprised nor should the students.

I have not put a grade on a paper for the past twenty-five years, of my now thirty-six years of teaching. And I haven't given an examination in any traditional sense for twenty-three years. During that time, I have taught courses involving college students, freshmen through doctoral level, as well as juniors and seniors in high school. While I have worked with a variety of grading patterns (which were part of the conventions in the institutions), in most of those years letter grades (*A, B, C, D, F*) existed and had to be given at the end of a marking period (in a high school setting) and at the end of each semester in the university.

While I can't say that I have worked it all out intellectually and emotionally, I have come to the point of feeling reasonably comfortable with my ways of dealing with classroom evaluation. I start always with the premise that *each* student will be successful—and, in fact, that I am as responsible as the student for making sure that our experience together is successful. My instructional approaches are built around that premise. I make my expectations clear:

> That students will participate in discussion and shared learning efforts (I structure many different settings to ensure ease of participation: small-group activities, cooperative learning projects, formal and informal presentations, and conferences; I also root as much of the writing as possible around personal observations, reflections, understandings, and inquiries).
>
> That journals will be maintained and focused on observations, reading, classroom discussions, and extensions of thought (I read and interact with students carefully around these journals, providing encouragement, posing questions, and in many ways setting standards).
>
> That all reading that I assign will be read carefully and thoughtfully, noted in their journals, used in their more formal writing, and commented on in discussion (I tend to assign a modest amount of reading to make clear my intent on deep reading and thought).
>
> That additional books and articles, selected by students, will be read and shared (from bibliography that I provide as well as related sources that the students come across).
>
> That the formal writing (generally six pieces each semester, mostly five to eight pages at the university level, two to

four pages at the high school level) will assume in most cases a personal stance and be taken seriously (and always read by me carefully and responded to dialogically and in detail).

That a final synthesis will be produced (in writing or orally).

Typically, students begin at many different points. Their background experience tends to differ, their confidence levels are diverse, their willingness to take a personal stance on any content is uneven. I share with students my expectations that they will *progress* over the semester in relation to the quality of their writing, thought, and participation, that their understandings will deepen.

What I find is that students tend to go far beyond my expectations or theirs. They don't ask along the way, "What did I get?" and "How am I doing?" The depth of my responses along the way in writing and in verbal exchange generally provides them with sufficient understanding of their progress. I believe they come to understand that we are working together.

But then a grade has to be given! I ask myself in relation to all students, what has their progress been? Did they fulfill every assignment, complete all expectations? Generally, based on such deliberation, most students receive an *A* or *B*. Students who don't get an *A* or *B* typically get an incomplete and a time period to finish work or rework what they have done. These students won't get more than a *B* and many will likely receive *C* grades. (I would prefer using only Credit or Pass.) Seldom in twenty-five years have I had a student ask about a final grade—why a *B* or a *C* and not an *A*. Concerns about grades have been put far into the background; learning has been placed in the foreground.

Thus far I have focused my remarks on classroom evaluation, related principally to *grading* and the myriad of individual activities students engage in. But evaluation is obviously more than that. Our concern about the growth of our students should cause us as teachers to be attentive to the classroom environments we create, the materials we use, the questions we raise, the overall attitudes we express, the learning climate we promote—in other words, the *surround* for student learning. (My good friend Lillian Weber introduced me to the word "surround" used in this way. I like the breadth that it conveys.) Our need for reflection on our practices (analogous to the self-evaluation I suggested was so important for students) is great.

Beyond our self-reflection, how do we get other constructive responses to our work? While most school systems have mandatory teacher evaluations, typically conducted by principals, they tend to be narrow in their scope, much too ritualized, and generally superficial. Few teachers speak of these evaluation systems as particularly powerful or helpful. (In many respects they are surrounded by the same problems as student evaluation and grading.)

Depending on the ages of our students, we can periodically ask them to respond to the quality of the educational experiences we are providing—the questions we raise, the pedagogical approaches we employ, the materials we make available, the evaluation processes we use. Such efforts affirm the mutuality of the educational encounter, the sense that we are in this together.

Inviting other teachers to observe occasionally, asking them to focus on an aspect of practice we wonder about, can also be productive. Also useful is systematic journal writing, in which attention is paid to aspects of our largest purposes, to unusual questions raised by students, to the circumstances surrounding unusually successful and unsuccessful activities, followed by focused conversations with colleagues.

A number of years ago, I worked in settings where parents were active and played, on occasion, an evaluative role. Because the parents thought their classroom observations would be enhanced with some kind of guide, we worked together on a series of questions for that purpose. Teachers at the time found the questions engaging, and over the years, many teachers have been using them for self-evaluation purposes. While they were aimed at elementary classrooms, I believe they have potential beyond that level. Several of the questions follow.

Classroom approaches are good if they help children learn.
- When you visit the school, watch the children. Are they interested? Are they involved? Are they learning?

- Do the teachers, aides, and children like each other?
- Are the teachers and aides doing most of the talking?
- Do teachers, aides, and children listen to each other?
- Are they learning from each other?
- Do they respect each other?
- Does learning start with children's interests?
- Do the walls show children's work? Or the teacher's?
- Does the setting allow children to solve their own problems or answer their questions in a number of ways?

Reading is particularly important.
- Is reading an important activity?
- Are there large numbers of books? Do children have easy access to reading materials?
- Do the teachers like reading?

School should be a happy place.
- Are teachers and aides happy to be in the school?
- Are children happy to be in this school? Do they like what they are doing?
- Is there evidence of art, music, dance?
- Is every child treated with respect?
- Do children help each other? Or is competition encouraged?
- Do children talk to one another and to adults?
- Is the classroom bright, interesting to look at, a nice place to be?

Schools often have many new materials and equipment.
- Do children have access to all the materials and equipment? Do they actively use the materials?
- Is everything paper, pencil, and books? Or are there materials to touch, manipulate, build?
- Are there materials that encourage exploration?

Good questions? I think so! Can you watch children and tell if they're interested in their school activities? If they like to read? I meet few parents or teachers (and many of the teachers are also parents) who have difficulty with such observations. If children aren't interested, teachers certainly have a problem to which they need to attend.

Evaluation is undeniably complex. It is also important. Thought about through individual as well as collective reflection, it can assume more constructive directions.

Seven

Matters of Accountability

In this chapter I address issues of evaluation that relate to public accountability as well as to classroom practice. Very little of what now occurs on the accountability side of evaluation, guided mostly by standardized tests of one kind or another, appears particularly useful to students. In fact, it works too often to the disadvantage of many, contributing to considerable retention, inappropriate special education placements, and other forms of tracking, as well as to limitations on the range of learning experiences that are made available.

The various state and local district accountability systems, built almost entirely around standardized tests, may well have been constructed with good intentions and a belief that they would contribute to better schools, but they have led in practice to considerable discouragement among teachers and students. It is *always* difficult to pursue powerful ends when such discouragement prevails.

Regardless of what apologists for these various tests may say, and there are many who remain willing to believe that the problems have been exaggerated, the cost of this testing tends to be very high. And the cost is not just economic; it is also time, a far more valuable commodity. I watch children in many elementary schools engaged in practice for tests by the hours over periods of weeks, sometimes months. Rather than reading real books during these practice periods, children read isolated paragraphs with multiple-choice questions that are essentially facsimiles of tests. They work on math worksheets that are also facsimiles of tests. And in secondary schools, they learn strategies for dealing with analogies or reading passages, what students suggest are the "tricks" related to various standardized tests. To think of the educational process as "tricks" is to encourage cynicism.

If preparing for these tests seems wasteful, it becomes even more so when we realize that they provide *meagre* information of worth to teachers. They have almost no diagnostic value and add little to teachers' knowledge of students. They certainly don't help teachers with the question, What should I do to help this or that student learn?

Even as test scores rise as a result of increased teaching to the tests (which should be expected), the quality of the educational experience appears in many settings to be stagnating. One indication is that rising test scores are no longer matters for public applause. As one case in point, tests scores in New York City have been going up for a decade, with averages well above national norms, and yet the popular view is that the schools are in a state of collapse, offering too little substantial education to their students. Nationally, almost every school district and state now reports above-average scores on most testing programs, yet there is little public belief that the schools are doing well, that there has been any large-scale improvement.

Policymakers at all levels, however, are beginning to rethink the way accountability systems work, understanding increasingly that they reduce the decision-making potential of those in schools and may well be influencing negatively the directions of curricular and pedagogical practices. This is providing an opening for teachers to develop at the school level accountability processes worthy of the name, processes that are rooted principally in their instructional programs, not apart from them, and which can benefit students as they inform teachers.

We need to engage in assessment that is rooted more directly in the instructional process itself as well as being related to the best practice. In regard to this, I want to share the way a group of teachers in New York City responded to a new citywide science test for use in grades three and five. I believe the example is instructive for other assessment areas as well.

These teachers argued that *the* test (not assessment itself) was inappropriate for use in their classrooms, that it "covered too much ground too superficially" and didn't get close to what children actually knew and understood, that it didn't honor their slower, more intense, meaning-making, hands-on, observational, and experience-oriented approaches to science, and was a distraction at a time when serious science inquiry was becoming well established (Chittenden, 1986). Working with a research psychologist at the Educational Testing Service (ETS), the teachers developed a science assessment that used the district's objectives and the questions asked on the citywide test but made the basic questions open-ended. They wanted to demonstrate the larger possibilities through a less restricted process.

In the document they prepared as part of their proposal they wrote: "The multiple-choice format . . . allows no room for pupils to construct or generate answers based upon their knowledge and thought. . . . Further, tests which consist solely of questions for which there is only one correct response constitute an inappropriate assessment or model for science education. We are concerned that testing in this form will undercut science as a process, the investigative, experimental components of our science program which entail observation, experiment, and field work" (Chittenden, 1986, p. 4).

The citywide test asked: "Which of the following trees can be found growing along the streets of our city? (a) Redwood, (b) Palm, (c) Rubber, (d) Maple." In their alternative test the teachers asked, "Name some trees that grow along the streets of New York." The thirty third-grade children who took the alternative test named seventy-three different species of trees (including the "Central Park tree"). The city test asked "Which of the following planets is the largest? (a) Venus, (b) Mars, (c) Pluto, (d) Jupiter." The test prepared by the teachers asked students to draw a picture of the solar system. The drawings were enormously revealing.

The teachers and the ETS researcher didn't argue that the questions they asked were particularly appropriate, fully generative, connected to issues they believed were critical. They did conclude, however, that their open-ended process provided information more useful to classroom instruction and got closer to children's understandings than the multiple-choice, citywide test. For instructional purposes, teachers gained entry points they hadn't thought about.

Assessment for purposes that go beyond the school, and that is what most current accountability efforts are about, often means testing every child. Such assessment, however, doesn't need to function on an *individual* basis. This, too, needs greater acknowledgment. If taken seriously, it would alter the options. More open-ended, performance-oriented processes, what is increasingly being defined as "authentic assessment," for example, would likely be seen as more feasible if sampling were to be used. It could also involve the teachers in schools more directly rather than being a process owned and operated by some distant bureaucracy.

The *Abitur* in Germany is worth examining. It is an accountability assessment in which the largest share of the questions and problems (which always have multiple possibilities for response) are prepared by the classroom teachers in a school. The scoring and interpretation are also completed by classroom teachers. The results from all schools in a district are then compiled and reported.

Some of the most interesting performance-based assessment I have seen has been in use in England for the past ten years (and in South Australia more recently). The Assessment Performance Unit (APU) is intended for classroom use and has an interactive quality; in this sense it stands in sharp contrast to our silent, clock-bound, all-materials-off-the-desks, number 2 pencil formats. The assessor probes, prompts, even teaches in order to get close to what the students understand. The following comes from an APU test protocol (Wiggins, 1989, p. 709):

> [*The problem being explored in this sample relates to estimating the length of the circumference of a circle.*]
>
> *Ask:* "What would you do to check your estimate?" (String is on the table.) If no response, prompt for the string.
>
> *Ask:* "Is there any other method?" If student does not

suggest using $c = \pi d$, prompt with, "Would it help
to measure the diameter of the circle?"

The scoring is based on the assessor's determination of
"aided success" or "unaided success."

The point of all of this is that we do know how to engage
in the kinds of assessment that make it possible to keep integrity in
our various instructional programs and also provide information to
the public. To make this point more clear, I would like to draw
from the area of writing because work here represents the most
serious break yet in the power of standardized testing. Those concerned about writing in the schools have been increasingly convincing in their arguments that writing cannot be assessed validly
outside the instructional process itself and that writing to a real
audience is central. They have been articulate in their arguments
that writing at its best is *situated* and thus not easily standardized
in current psychometric or technological terms. I would like to
share the experience other teachers and I have had with writing
assessment.

It is clear that understanding children's and young people's
writing cannot begin with a single piece of work or with writing
that has not been completed within the norms of ongoing and
thoughtful classroom practice. That approach isn't likely to bring
forth students' best and most committed efforts. Such an understanding alone has significantly changed the assessment landscape.

Teachers who are encouraging active writing programs make
clear that serious writing takes thought and time. It is not unsituated, far removed from personal experience or interest, unconnected
to an individual's way of interpreting the world. They recognize
that in settings where the ongoing school experience of the students
is rich, where teachers read a great deal to children, giving emphasis
to authorship and personal style, where books are plentiful, where
active learning is promoted, where the world is permitted to in-
trude, to blow through the classroom, children have *much more* to
talk and write about. In this sense, writing is not something apart;
it has a context and that context is important to understanding the
writing that is actually produced. Most writing assessment efforts
that have existed provide little knowledge of contextual issues.

Experience has also shown that the best person to judge particular students' writing, who can address constructively their progress as writers, their writing biographies as it were, is the teacher closest to them. That shouldn't surprise anyone. It is the classroom teacher who knows, for example, the questions a particular child has been raising about various aspects of classroom learning, and can refer, when reading a piece of writing, to previous pieces of writing, to the particular book the child is currently reading, to the genres or authors that the child is most inclined toward at the moment, to a painting just completed, to a trip recently taken, to the new baby sister in the home, to the spring flooding across the community's many glacial lake beds, to the special meadow colors, to the classroom's human mosiac. This teacher's reading eye and thought can be responsive to the surrounding context, never really separate from the text. As a result, the teacher can bring an interpretation that has meaning. It is that teacher, deeply involved with the child as writer, who knows the next question to raise, when to push and when not to, who can judge the meaning and quality of a piece. It is this outlook, by the way, that governs my perspective about evaluation issues as a whole.

This all becomes clear when reading children's work in the various publications of the Teachers and Writers Collaborative (see Murphy, 1974, and Landrum, 1971) or the accounts prepared by Don Graves (1983) and Lucy Calkins (1983). And I see similarly impressive writing in large numbers of elementary and secondary schools where active writing programs have been established.

As I read this remarkable writing, knowing as I do that each of the pieces was completed over time, not at one sitting, not without conversation, not without several tries, not without some peer response and early teacher response, I wonder what would have been produced had these writers been forced to write on April 1 at 10:00 A.M., knowing they had thirty minutes and the readers would be persons far away. (Actually I don't wonder too much. I have seen the writing and it isn't the same. And teachers I know don't believe that students' writing on those days represents anything approximating their best work. Many of the students, in fact, leave much of the writing assessment page blank—and they are often the most skilled writers.)

Teachers who honor children's and young people's work as genuine products of thought capable of evoking thought in others can certainly describe their students' writing. They are authentic readers. And they have been convincing in their views that any talk of assessment that doesn't understand the importance of being close to the student writer and the surrounding context is doomed intellectually.

So where does this lead us regarding an assessment program? Since we have already acknowledged the centrality of the classroom setting, the classroom teacher, and work over time, the principal direction should be obvious enough. It is rooted in carefully organized and considered classroom documentation. Classroom teachers can, for example, systematically preserve copies of drafts of students' writing as well as finished pieces. Three or four pieces a month would provide a reasonable collection. Such a collection is the base for what is being called in this new evaluation environment a "portfolio." Reviewing these portfolios periodically can inform a teacher's ongoing efforts to assist particular students. And, of course, this is an important purpose of such documentation.

At year's end, the accumulation, organized chronologically, can be subjected to careful review with some of the following questions serving as a framework. Over time what are the salient features and dominant motifs? How much invention? What about complexity? Choice of topics? Discourse frameworks? Connections to ongoing academic and social strengths? Diversity of word use? Voice? Use of conventions?

Such a review can be especially revealing, often providing a perspective missed in the course of addressing work that stands alone. Such a portfolio is almost always revealing to parents, bringing the kind of overview, that large picture, that parents often miss as they interact with their children about the school experience.

This kind of classroom-based review can also address concerns about the ongoing support of individual students and it can inform further ongoing instructional practice. It can also serve as a way for a teacher to describe students' growth as writers over the course of a year as well as inform more fully the children's subsequent teacher or teachers. In addition, having collections of work over time can assist the students themselves in bringing careful self-evaluation and more solid interpretation to their own efforts as writers. Such an opportunity ought not to be missed.

For purposes of a larger schoolwide review, randomly selected students from each classroom in a school might be asked to select five or six pieces of their writing to be read by groups of teachers in the school as a whole—providing the readers with a statement of context for the individual works. At the level of the school, using such samples as a base, knowing that they were written within the instructional program itself and not apart from it, not a forced, unsituated exercise, should provide readers with more confidence about describing, for example, the writing of fourth-graders in this Thomas Jefferson Elementary School. And they should be able to do it with good authority.

Further, by forming in the school "a community of readers of writing," the teachers involved in this schoolwide review can actually enlarge their own understandings of writing, very likely becoming in the process better teachers and facilitators of writing. If evaluation doesn't produce such results, it is quite clearly a failed and faulty exercise.

Having argued that the most appropriate evaluation is classroom- and school-based, it is still possible to extend the logic of making use of multiple samples, embedded in best practice, to a school system where a community of readers linked to shared beliefs can be formed. With each step away from the classroom, however, confidence levels must, of necessity, begin to decline. With that, I want to share two somewhat unusual assessment efforts conducted by school districts. Neither was aimed at individuals. While both accept a good deal of conventional practice, they have reconstructed the possibilities in fairly rich ways.

The first comes from Ann Arbor, Michigan. In 1983, quite apart from teachers, their wishes, their approach to writing, or their beliefs about writing and the ways it ought to be taught, the district made a decision to contract with a national testing enterprise to assess writing in the three high schools. The testing company handled all aspects of the assessment. On the appointed day for assessment, students were given a writing prompt and were provided forty minutes to produce a writing sample. The whole affair proved problematical and disruptive. Many of the students refused, as it turned out, to participate. A report was produced which teachers argued had no meaning.

In the aftermath, several English teachers who had for a number of years been deeply involved with a variety of national writing projects stressing process approaches presented a proposal to the superintendent and school board in which they argued eloquently that no assessment could be credible if it didn't model the best hopes of the instructional process itself. In this sense they were arguing for a theory-based assessment. To their surprise, they were given the contract—released time for meetings, summer stipends to plan and write, and some secretarial assistance. They interviewed their colleagues about writing practices, read student writing together, tried out a variety of assessment activities that were congruent with their actual writing programs, and wrote responses to the various assessment prompts they were considering. They also involved from the outset their students who came to feel a sense of shared community between themselves as student-writers and their teachers as reader-evaluators.

The final prompt, revolving around an issue of "fairness," a personal topic that invited a first-person, informal style, was selected cooperatively by students and faculty. The assessment itself involved all eleventh-graders—1,035 of them. And it was carried out over several days in the ongoing instructional mode, which included prewriting, conversation, peer-group work, data gathering, drafting, and revision. All English teachers in the system were involved in the holistic reading around criteria they had worked out. There were three readers for each paper. Students received their papers back—an unusual feature for such evaluations—and their teachers, who were a part of the process, discussed the scores and their meanings.

It was not perfect, but these teachers carried off a writing assessment that was interesting for students, occurred within and not apart from their instructional programs, and created a circumstance that enabled them to enlarge their learning about writing and its possibilities.

The second example comes from Grand Forks, North Dakota, where the superintendent of schools agreed to a classroom-based, instructionally oriented writing assessment to be planned by teachers. Grade six was selected as the focus. The teachers began by examining samples of children's writing together. Further, they read collectively books and articles by Don Graves (1983); Lucy Calkins (1983); Jerome Harste, Virginia Woodward, and Carolyn Burke (1984); and James Britton (1970, 1975). They learned about the diverse ways sixth-grade teachers throughout the system worked with writing and they themselves also became deeply enmeshed in the kind of writing workshop that Don Graves and Lucy Calkins suggest. Documenting their own practices, reflecting together on their experiences, and reading work produced by their children in the workshop setting together helped them bring a constructive outlook on the districtwide mandate for assessment. It also helped them get close to children's writing and informed their ongoing practice productively.

For the assessment study, they decided not to use a prompt but to ask students to complete a personal narrative of their own choosing, within the framework of the ongoing instruction. In classrooms where a process approach existed, that was the structure; in other settings, different processes prevailed. Six hundred and fifty narratives were produced. A holistic process, using as criteria clear message, logical sequence, voice, and mechanics, enabled the teachers to respond descriptively and quantitatively to the question "How well do sixth-graders in the Grand Forks public schools write?"

While the process had some limitations, it was embedded within classroom practice, enlarged school-systemwide discussion about writing and writing process, provided teachers with more experience as readers of written discourse, and broadened insights into the teaching of writing.

In both Ann Arbor and Grand Forks, communities of writing teachers, persons who can link the teaching of writing to the classroom context and understand ways to make connections between writing and evaluation, are being formed. This is empowerment of a high order. In addition, and I can't give enough stress to this, because of the ways the evaluation process was organized, large numbers of students in these two settings have been provided experience evaluating their own writing. All this will contribute more to improving writing in the schools than will any process that stands apart from teachers and their ongoing instructional efforts in classrooms.

Finally, I wish to offer one more entry into the arena of accountability; it is essentially a means for building greater teacher authority over, and more control of, the accountability process. It is a means of doing more of what has been suggested thus far in this chapter.

I start from the premise that teachers and schools need to communicate clearly to parents, students, and their respective school communities what their large purposes are, including, of course, attention to the common basic skills and expressive arts fields; how they propose organizing to support those purposes; how they plan to ensure students' growth in relation to the purposes; and how they will report to parents. The school's statement will likely be more general than the statement prepared by a classroom teacher.

The teacher's statement should address these issues: intentions (purposes) for the year; general direction of the curriculum; topics, ideas, activities to be given primary attention; and expectations. The statement might also include a description of the classroom, the kinds of materials that will be made available, and the teacher's point of view about learning. A statement that invites the parents' active participation, a *genuine* wish to stay in touch with them for the benefit of their children, should also be included, and should be followed during the year by frequent efforts to communicate.

While these remarks are not directly related to evaluation for purposes of accountability, they are connected. They speak to issues of communication, letting parents and students know what you have in mind for the year. Done thoughtfully, this statement will go a long way toward building parent and student confidence (which is partially what accountability is about).

The statement I am suggesting would also have an evaluation section. It would include a point of view about the *importance* of evaluation, especially as a means of getting close to the curricular understandings, strengths, interests, and academic and social learning of the students. It would also include information about how evaluation will proceed and records of performance maintained, along with ways parents will be kept informed.

If the school uses standardized tests, the teacher might make clear what purpose these tests play, and in what ways they affect their children. A statement expressing your point of view about the tests might also prove instructive, the beginning of a productive exchange.

Evaluation is important for growth. It needs more serious attention. As now practiced, developed in large measure around a host of standardized tests, accountability has increasingly come to mean *no* accountability. While I give in this chapter considerable attention to fresh developments in the area of writing, most of what is outlined could be applied to most other areas of learning as well.

Eight

Empowering Teachers

I first began to use the phrase "teacher empowerment" in the late 1960s, though I knew at the time that it had roots going back into the nineteenth century, particularly in relation to the active teacher reading groups within and among schools (especially in rural areas) and the child study movement, with its attention to teacher research. In resurrecting the conception, I was responding, in part, to the so-called teacherproof curriculum materials that were being developed during some of these years, what I saw as a direction that would ultimately take the heart and soul out of teaching. Turning teachers into technicians, intermediaries for someone else's ideas and curriculum, with little concern for local circumstances, seemed very poor policy then. My views haven't changed.

For me, teaching has always meant decision making about curriculum, materials, and pedagogy. As a teacher in the schools, it had never occurred to me that I should, or had to, ask permission to use particular materials, choose not to use a textbook, rearrange the furniture, or make use of diverse community resources. I assumed it was my responsibility to develop what I considered the most appropriate curriculum for the students with whom I worked (though I did understand, of course, that I should be able to explain my actions and my purposes and their relationships to the learning of the students in my classes).

I learned rather quickly that my outlook was not altogether common. Still, it seemed to me that if teachers lacked such basic decision-making authority, schools could not possibly get better, and the people we most needed as teachers would likely choose to do other things. From a historical perspective, as I discuss more fully in Chapter Eleven, it is not surprising that we have been most successful in recruiting large numbers of particularly talented, intellectually able individuals into teaching during our more progressive periods, when teacher decision making was most encouraged.

Teacher empowerment, as I will develop it, is closely related to the issue of authority, but not the vested authority growing from a person's position in some hierarchy or social status. It grows from the real authority that comes from knowledge, understanding, wisdom, and control of the guiding language and craft of teaching. It is mostly about professionalism writ large. As a formulation it stems from an acknowledgment that the considerable intellectual and moral power that teachers possess needs to assume more dominance in schools.

As teacher empowerment is spoken about presently (and the conception is, I believe, being used in so many ways and so indiscriminately that it is losing its vitality), it is increasingly being tied to participation in decision making in relation to school governance (around school-site management), as well as to negotiated control over aspects of teaching in the schools (planning time, calendar issues, and meeting schedules). This isn't to say that authoritativeness in connection with purposes, curriculum, and pedagogy has been forgotten. But at the level of schools, even those that have linked teacher empowerment with school restructuring, that isn't the predominant discourse surrounding the formulation of empowerment.

I start from the premise that teachers and principals and parents, in *particular* schools, must be the principal decision makers about the appointment of new teachers, budgets, schedules, materials, curriculum, evaluation, discipline and attendance policies, student assignment mechanisms, and social service arrangements. Such shared decision making is basic to democratic schooling. I also believe collective thought about these schoolwide issues needs ongoing nurturance and support. But these shared leadership and decision-making processes are, at their best, more an outcome of teacher empowerment, of acknowledged needs for cooperative action on behalf of the students, of collective interests in pursuing larger purposes, than necessarily a beginning point.

Though it is clearly related, having a prescribed role in a governance process fully defined externally, which is now the convention, doesn't necessarily translate into the productive empowerment that I am pursuing here. The biggest decision made by the governance body in a school in a highly touted school-site management, "teacher empowerment" school district over a recent two-year period, as reported by administrators and teachers, was to "decrease class periods by four minutes and increase the lunch period by fifteen minutes." In this district, the contract mandated a role for teachers in school decision making through representation on governance committees. In most schools in the district it is a ho-hum affair. Truly empowering activities just don't exist.

I encourage teachers everywhere to begin at the outset of their careers to develop serious professional relationships and establish practices that will further their learning, that will enlarge their authoritativeness, and, in the process, provide them a more powerful voice and greater freedom of action. From my experience, teachers themselves need to take many of the first steps. They can't wait for universities, foundations, the business community, or various school administrators, though all these external agencies and individuals can make important contributions.

While I had concerns in the 1960s that caused me to think about teacher empowerment and begin to work intensively to help teachers develop more constructive professional learning environments for themselves, as they ensured powerful learning for children and young people, the dilemmas have grown larger. This has especially been the case for the past decade and a half. We have seen, for example, a huge increase in state legislation governing curriculum, and the pressures to narrow school practices have increased substantially.

The difficulties associated with the new narrowness come through clearly in Shirley Brice-Heath's *Ways with Words: Language, Life, and Work in Communities and Classrooms* (1983), a powerful account of literacy and people's voices rooted in Appalachia. Brice-Heath outlines how teachers who had learned to be ethnographers of language (an empowering direction) brought the strength of the diverse languages in children's homes and communities into the schools. This concentration on language was designed to help children, who also had been taught to be ethnographers of language, connect their familiar ways of knowing with the more unfamiliar ways embedded in the standard curriculum. Brice-Heath describes supportive language classrooms in which rich narrative flowed, cooperative exploration of how language was used was encouraged, and communities and their language strengths became more fully respected. Expectations hadn't been dulled through any early identification and tracking of children as language deficient because they used nonstandard forms. These, of course, are the kinds of educational settings we need everywhere.

But the book closed on a discouraging note—the teacher-ethnographers associated with Brice-Heath's research in the early 1970s either left teaching or quit in place. She quotes one representative teacher: "My district requires me to give criterion referenced tests, then teach each student on the basis of the profile of needed subsets of skills which come back on a computer printout. . . . They run everyone through the same hierarchy of learning. . . . There is little time any more for serious language work" (pp. 356–357). It is sad to read, but increasingly it is becoming a commonplace refrain.

Not so long ago, the associate superintendent of schools of one of the nation's largest urban districts shared with me how successful they had become by standardizing almost every aspect of curriculum. (Success meant increasing standardized test scores.) Children in grades one through three, she noted, learn to write sentences and in grades four through six, they learn about paragraphs. In the primary grades, every teacher is required to have on the board each day a sentence that begins with a lower-case letter and doesn't have a period or question mark at the end. And each day, the corrections are made. Children come to know, I was told, that sentences begin with capital letters and end with a symbol of some sort. I asked whether it had been difficult to get teacher compliance to such a program. She said it had been extremely difficult "but *finally* teachers do it." Programs such as this don't encourage authoritativeness among teachers.

In hearings associated with the National Coalition of Advocates for Students report, *Barriers to Excellence* (1985), there was a good deal of testimony about reading programs that made use of few books, either commercial or student written. Teachers talked about controlled vocabulary systems produced on cards in the form of short sentences and paragraphs. Such programs are also not associated with confident, articulate, knowledgeable teachers who have been encouraged and supported to be powerful or to maintain large visions of possibilities for children.

In one school district in which a colleague completed a curriculum review, the following textbooks were used in all the third grades: a math book, a math workbook, a reading book, a reading workbook, a science book, a science workbook, a social studies book, a social studies workbook, a health book, a health workbook, a handwriting workbook, a spelling workbook, a language arts book, and a language arts workbook. The days were spent opening and closing books at fairly regular ten- and twenty-minute intervals. Teachers were, for the most part, technicians, giving lots of instructions but doing very little teaching as teaching has been understood traditionally. Powerful learning, confronting rich language, the exploration of natural materials, significant conversation were missing dimensions.

I must acknowledge that the current disempowering pressures are as great as they have ever been. Nonetheless, based on considerable personal experience as well as what I take from the accounts of others, those teachers who maintain their sense of personal authority tend not to be as limited by external pressures. They are able, even in difficult times, to make personal decisions about curriculum and instructional practices and are more able, as a result, to organize classrooms that challenge children through their diversity and rich array of materials and possibilities.

The authority that I am acknowledging here emerges from sound knowledge gained from close observation of children, systematic reflection on practice, and immersion into the descriptive literature of teaching, philosophical and historical. Such knowledge leads to a firm, internalized control of the language related to one's craft and can be a base for learning with others, a breaking through the isolation so endemic in schools.

John Dewey offered several points of entry for us to consider in our thinking about teacher empowerment. He noted early in his writing that the schools, whether they focused on the primary grades or the university level, needed to be staffed by scholars and not technicians. Scholars, he wrote, were "full of the spirit of inquiry," investigators who posed interesting questions, who explored new ways of thinking about the world.

Dewey used the notion of "students of teaching" as his way of describing empowered teachers, people not dependent on decisions made externally by those far removed from the reality of a particular setting. To be a student of teaching in his terms was to establish and maintain a reflective capacity and to become articulate about one's intentions. He might ask a teacher:

- Why do you organize that way and not another?
- Why that array of materials and not another?
- What are you leading toward and why?
- What are these particular experiences leading toward?
- How does learning activity in one area make a connection to learning activities in another?
- How do your provisioning decisions promote community building as they support individual growth?
- How are the different inclinations of each student in the room being supported?
- How do you know that important growth is occurring?

Control over such questions was seen by Dewey as a critical base for being in a position to make independent judgments about one's classroom. There was, as he thought about it, no room for saying, "I don't know what's happening or how to gain access to what's happening," no room for an inability to speak intelligently and clearly about practice.

Anne Bussis, Edward Chittenden, and Marianne Amarel, in *Beyond Surface Curriculum* (1976), elaborate on Dewey's point in their response to the question: How important is it for teachers to be able to analyze, reflect upon, and articulate their basic assumptions about teaching?

It seems to us that analysis and articulation of the
teaching/learning environment are important in at
least two respects. First, analysis and articulation are
critical components of the teacher's ability to communicate to others; to administrators, to parents, to
other teachers (and, in a much more subtle and complex way, to children). . . . But second, and less commonly discussed, analysis would seem important for a
teacher's evaluation of his/her own efforts—especially
when things start to go poorly or to stagnate. What
conscious frame of reference can the teacher bring to
bear in an attempt to analyze what is happening? Can
he/she look at the relationship of curricular concerns
to surface content . . . and begin to sort out priorities?
[pp. 6–7].

Dewey, Bussis, Chittenden, and Amarel are essentially placing the power of *reflection* before us, that process of stepping back,
looking again, gaining added perspective and insight, greater understanding. Reflection of this kind can occur through individual
or group thought.

In many schools, teachers have come together for group reflection on particular children, materials, ideas, and patterns. Patricia Carini, who has pioneered group reflection processes so
effectively, describes reflection as "turning thinking back on myself.
When I reflect, I hold my own thinking in front of me, as if it were
an objective aspect of myself viewed in a mirror. . . . Reflection is
thinking which gathers, keeps and preserves thought by finding the
pattern of relationship among seemingly disparate events. It is a
special branch of remembering which consciously chooses a focus
to concentrate on—a subject which may be an idea, an image, a
motif, a symbol, an experience, a person, [or] an event" (Carini,
1979, p. 30).

Let me bring more concreteness to this. Many teachers have
found daily journal writing, rooted in their classroom observations,
to be particularly informative, a means of getting closer to their
practice and to children's learning. These efforts usually begin very
slowly, often painfully, yielding in the early stages a lot of white

space on the pages. The longer teachers stay with it, however, the more they try to bring some focus to their observations, the more detailed their descriptions become, the more connections they are able to make.

Teachers generally find it helpful to begin their journals around such guiding questions as "What were the important things that happened in the classroom today?" or "What went well in mathematics and why?" They move on from there to observations of particular children over time, trying to gain greater insights into their preferences, their questions, their particular understandings, in the process learning more about all children. In many cases, they move from description of this kind to questions leading to focused inquiries; for example, "What occurred today that caused me to wonder, that I didn't understand clearly?" or "Why is there so much dependence on me?" or "Why do I get so little imaginative writing?" or "What did I do a little of that I would like to do more of? What prevented me from doing that?"

Maintaining a journal is, without question, very difficult, in large measure because time is always short. But it is also difficult because we don't tend to see ourselves as writers, or we don't really believe we need to write to reflect on our work. In regard to the latter, teachers have told me, "I reflect on my teaching while I drive home, mow the lawn, do the dishes, take an evening walk." I believe that is true for many teachers, but it likely is never as productive as thinking *and* writing. Teachers who engage in journal writing for a period of time (a few months, a year, and more) do become better observers of their students and their practices. They also become more reflective and grow in their ability to speak clearly and authoritatively about their craft. The benefits are high.

These journals and related inquiry efforts, what are being seen as beginning teacher-as-researcher activities, have often led to shared activities exemplified by the Children's Thinking Seminars described so well by William Hull (1978) and Kathe Jervis (1979). These are systematic efforts of teachers who come together on a regular basis in an effort to enlarge their personal and collective understandings of children's thinking and growth as learners. Such reflective activities can lead to teachers inquiring more deeply into their practice. For purposes of practical illustration, I'll share two fairly straightforward inquiry activities in which I was involved with a team of five teachers who were learning how to reflect on their practice together. I share them as examples of teachers at fairly early stages of trying to become more serious students of teaching.

The group began discussing the importance of questions, believing that *why* questions were particularly critical for extending children's learning vertically as well as horizontally. As a way of thinking about this more concretely, the teachers worked out a means to monitor the questions of children and themselves for a week. To their dismay, *where, what, when,* and *how* questions were overwhelmingly dominant in the classrooms. They wondered whether such factors as classroom organization, curriculum, and their own practices had anything to do with the kinds of questions that dominated the classrooms. They noted the following: Materials tended to be stored away in relatively inaccessible places. Books, other than those housed in the school library, were limited in variety and number. Worksheets and workbooks were used in association with almost every learning activity. Teachers organized themselves around "specializations" with children moving frequently from one teacher to another. Time was tightly scheduled. Art, for example, was precisely twenty minutes long from the teacher's introduction to the moment the children left for another activity.

Their analysis, essentially their reflective activity, led to a number of initial, though tentative, conclusions: open-ended questions were not encouraged in the circumstances under which they were teaching; the materials in use, demanding as they did precise ways of responding, encouraged, if anything, questions of *where, what, when,* and *how;* the reliance on worksheets and workbooks and the tight scheduling put the teacher in a role of giving frequent instructions that tended to be dominated by *when, where, what,* and *how;* dependence on the teachers in such an environment, as they determined, could hardly be avoided. One might argue that such understandings should have been obvious but, to teachers involved, it became more clear, more understandable when they actually engaged in a systematic process of documentation and analysis.

Another concern they chose to examine was related to "communication with parents." One documentation task was to record every personal or telephone contact they made with parents during a one-month period and then categorize them. Several things emerged. The contacts were numerous, averaging almost one per day. But most of the contacts they initiated were negative in tone, relating principally to particular children not performing well and being disruptive. Actually recording all the interactions and reflecting carefully on the data were informative and provided teachers an opportunity to discuss the implications. They caused them to consider calling *all* parents regularly, with a view toward more positive interactions.

As part of this general area of concern the teachers also brought together all formal written materials sent home to parents for a two-month period. They examined the documents and asked themselves: Are the communications personal in tone? Are they informative and educational about what is actually occurring in the classroom? Having all the communications together provided a different view, a broader perspective, than seeing only one or two. A large share of the communications were not signed by teachers (their names were typed only). Many carried designations such as "Team A teachers" rather than the names of the individual teachers. The communications were dominated—90 percent—by announcements about school activities in general (PTA meetings, lunch schedules, reminders to parents to have the children wear boots); they were not particularly informative about the classroom experiences of the children.

Both those activities were important starting points for enlarged understanding of their practices and for increased levels of empowerment. They represented beginning points for developing their school as a reflective community. Schools that have reflective cultures, places where ideas are thought about, where commonplace beliefs are held up to public discussion, are generally inspiring places intellectually and educationally. They are learning communities.

The teacher research of the sort I have described reminds me of William James's *Talks to Teachers on Psychology and to Students on Some of Life's Ideas* ([1899] 1958). The child study movement had taken hold near the end of the nineteenth century, and teachers were encouraged to become careful documenters of children's learning, to join in the descriptions that informed the growing field of psychology. While James supported the movement and believed "it is refreshing our sense of the child's life" (p. 12), he also went on to say, "But, for Heaven's sake, let the rank and file of teachers be passive readers if they so prefer, and feel free not to contribute to the accumulation [of records and accounts of children's language]. Let not the prosecution of [child study] be preached as an imperative duty. . . . The worst thing that can happen to a good teacher is to get a bad conscience about her progression because she feels hopeless as a psychologist. Our teachers are overworked already" (p. 13).

I agree fully that teachers should not feel guilty about not being psychologists. And it is true that teachers are generally overworked. But as they become more careful observers, systematically documenting aspects of their interactions and children's questions, the more they will take note of and the more thoughtful their teaching will become. If they join with others, discussing together their learning, they will be enriched even more.

Whether teachers engage in larger public writing is, of course, another matter. My hope would be that many would write, and in this way enrich the educational literature, possibly informing others of new questions, fresh ways of thinking about pedagogy, curriculum, and sources of development.

In the first decades of this century, it was common for teachers in the progressive schools to write about their experiences. (You might want to read work by such progressives as Harriet Johnson (1916), Marietta Johnson (1974), Grace Rotzel (1971), Agnes DeLima (1941), Margaret Naumberg (1928), Caroline Pratt (1948), and Julia Weber Gordon ([1946] 1970).) Fortunately, teachers are beginning to write again. What I have found most striking about much of the literature, whether associated with earlier or contemporary efforts, is the stress on reciprocity in relation to teachers' learning about children as well as about teaching. Stephen Rowland, a classroom teacher whom some of you may recognize as Michael Armstrong's collaborator in *Closely Observed Children* (1980), describes this reciprocity well in *Classroom Enquiry: An Approach to Understanding Children* (1984), a teacher-as-researcher presentation from which I provide a couple of paragraphs.

It takes considerable effort of the imagination to empathize with young children sufficiently to begin to understand their (individual) perspectives on the world. . . . But it is an effort which can reward us by stimulating and often challenging us to reconsider our own understanding.

I am reminded here of how my understanding of the concept, or operation, of subtraction was radically extended by considering how a group of seven-year-olds used seven different strategies for finding the difference between pairs of numbers all less than ten. Subtraction was a more diverse and more complex notion than I had initially thought. My claim here is not that these children's understanding of subtraction was greater than mine, but that their insights and their activity were sufficient to provoke me into reconsidering what I understood subtraction to be (p. 48–49).

I am reminded of a story from Lucianne Carmichael, author of *McDonogh 15* (1981), an extraordinary book about the making of a school in New Orleans. She tells of a five-year-old who insisted she come to the yard and stand with her under a tree whose yellowish leaves were falling. The child exclaimed, "Mrs. Carmichael, it's raining golden." That remark, one she had never heard before, brought a new understanding to Lucianne. The child had given her a real meaning that she could attach to the *golden rain tree,* which is the actual name of the tree.

I wish also to call your attention to a special philosophical, theoretical, and practical guide to teacher reflection and voice, a monograph of the North Dakota Study Group on Evaluation, *Speaking Out: Teachers and Teaching* (Traugh and others, 1986). The three paragraphs from the introduction speak, I believe, to the heart of any conception of reciprocity and teacher empowerment; in an implicit way they are at the base of my message:

This monograph is about our teaching practice—what it is and what it could be. It is about teachers—what we do and how we think about and learn from what is done. It is an exploration of a set of ideas about teaching—ideas which have a long history—which are made particular by our current, lived experience. Finally, and most importantly, it is about having a voice in what we do.

Having a voice is critical and political. We create, share, and change our world with and through language. Recognizing that day-to-day experience is a powerful source of understanding and knowledge which, when articulated, can be fed back into the quality of work is critical for teachers in gaining a voice. Recognizing knowledge and voicing it is basic to changing the ways teaching is thought about and enacted.

Voices, of course, need to be cultivated and supported. About 15 years ago, groups of teachers across the country started creating varying opportunities to lend each other the kinds of support needed to make themselves heard. For the teachers participating in this project, collegial groups . . . have been particularly important. They allowed teachers to talk about their practice and the children they teach, to describe both in some detail, and to help each other find the patterns and relationships, and thus meaning, within the wealth of detail of their teaching lives. These groups created space and time within which teachers could do this important thinking (pp. 4–5).

While I am recommending current books within this reciprocity—teacher empowerment—genre, I'll offer, in addition, *Inquiry into Meaning: An Investigation of Learning to Read* (1985) by Anne Bussis, Edward Chittenden, Marianne Amarel, and Edith Klausner, a collaborative research involving forty classroom teachers who not only noted an almost endless number of different ways in which children entered reading but also enlarged in the process their understandings of reading and the teaching of reading. Patricia Carini's *The Lives of Seven Children* (1984) also shows what it means to be engaged in close observation of children and their learning.

In making reference to books, I want to affirm the benefits of joint reading by groups of teachers, the opportunity for gaining fresh understandings of children, teaching, and the world, as well as intellectual stimulation through shared inquiry. You might in your own schools wish to consider a shared inquiry through one common book each semester. The book selected, however, should have some potential for challenging your ways of thinking about children, schools, and the society. Maxine Greene's *Landscapes of Learning* (1978) might be a good starting point.

With that, I want to return to John Dewey. He was particularly conscious of the power of social relationships, believing firmly that the development of intelligence and knowledge, whether for an individual or a culture, grew from cooperative exchange. The Dewey School prospered from the strength of its almost daily discussions about teaching and learning. In relation to this concern for interchange he wrote: "cooperation must . . . have a marked intellectual quality in the exchange of experience and ideas. Many of our early failures were due to the fact that our exchanges were too practical, too much given to matters of immediate import, and not sufficiently intellectual in content" (Mayhew and Edwards, [1936] 1966, p. 371).

You might want to think about that in regard to the school- and education-related meetings you attend. Groups I have worked with over the years have done far better when they didn't quickly get too practical, when they didn't feel compelled to finish discussing a book quickly, when they chose to understand issues deeply. The power, the real authority, that accrues for those with such experiences is substantial.

I want to pursue further the collaborative possibilities. Teachers in a number of schools have made cooperative decisions to organize around a semester-long or year-long schoolwide theme. Such efforts have provided another context for serious conversation, the sharing of resources, and cross-grade planning. It is another means for breaking through the isolation of teachers and students that is so endemic and enervating in so many of our schools.

Lillian Weber, a provocative teacher, philosopher, and as

passionate an advocate for democracy in schools as one could find in our field, pioneered the Open Corridor in New York City schools. It was an imaginative way of breaking big schools down into smaller units and creating common corridor spaces for activities involving children from several classrooms. But its largest purpose was to get teachers talking together about children, materials, and education. It was an empowering structural organization.

Where these kinds of collaborative efforts occur, teachers begin to see even more organizational possibilities, ways of meeting children better and articulating purposes more effectively. Schools desperately need fresh ideas, more structural and pedagogical possibilities. Toward that end, I often encourage those in and around schools to consider *what if* questions. What if we set aside forty-five minutes each day to read to children? What if painting, and dance, and music became again a central feature of our school from kindergarten through grade six? What if every teacher in our school scheduled one hour each day for a writing workshop rooted exclusively in children's experience, that grows out of children's thinking, that is not encumbered by any sentence starters, prompts, worksheets or workbooks, that gives attention to voice? What if at least three two-hour blocks of time each week were devoted to explorations in science rooted in observations of natural phenomena—the trees, shrubs, pond water, small animals, seeds, rocks, soils, flowers, various cooking ingredients? My purpose here is to suggest ways for groups of teachers to talk again about possibilities, to give relatively easy focus for shared inquiry.

I believe teachers ought to ask together how their individual schools and their classroom practices can meet students more appropriately and within a set of purposes that go beyond current definitions. In this regard, I was impressed several years ago when a teacher friend and colleague, who was part of a children's thinking seminar, was invited to join a districtwide committee to select a new basal reading series. Her refusal statement was impressive. She argued that a districtwide basal series was inappropriate, that at the least, each school should make a decision about texts— whether to use a series or not and if so, how. She also outlined how she believed reading should proceed; for her, any basal program to which she was expected to commit time and energy would be a retreat from good teaching. The response was, "You can do whatever you want—just make sure you keep parents well informed." That wasn't quite what she expected, or necessarily wanted.

Teachers need to express themselves about issues that matter educationally. Their voices in many communities have grown very dim. Empowered teachers consider themselves responsible for helping stimulate public discussion of important educational issues. They do this through letters to the editor, through guest viewpoint articles in the local press, through appearances on local radio programs relating to education, through classroom and school newsletters directed toward parents and other community members, through appearances before legislative committees, and through participation in policy statements about education made by teacher unions and political parties.

This leads me to a personal concern that would, I'm convinced, be resolved if teachers were more confident, more authoritative, more thoughtful and conscious observers. In the 1960s, for example, I did some writing for a civil rights group contesting the placement of Hispanics and blacks in special education. In a school district in which 20 percent of the students were Hispanic and black, over 70 percent of the students in special education were Hispanic and black. I was deeply disturbed that it was the parents, for the most part poorly educated Hispanic and black mothers, who asked how such a distribution was possible, *not* the teachers in the schools.

Though we continue to talk about taking individuals into account, acknowledging and respecting differences, recognizing a myriad of possibilities for learning, not wishing to place limits on individual development, tracking mechanisms have, nonetheless, grown in the schools, reaching today an unprecedented state. In the face of almost overwhelming evidence to the contrary, there persists a belief that separating students into ability groups is educationally beneficial or makes the teacher's tasks somehow easier. What is particularly and disturbingly *most* clear is that tracking and inequity are almost inextricable handmaidens. I won't argue that teachers are responsible for the level of tracking that exists, but they are certainly implicated.

The differences between upper and lower tracks of various courses are like night and day. Reading in many of the lower-track junior high courses I have observed rarely has anything to do with reading of books, or discussion, or writing. If a question is asked, "yes" or "no" is the answer sought. Students are not asked to think or communicate. Powerful teachers would be conscious of such practices and the language surrounding them, and they would seek remedies. Those in schools should begin to attune themselves to equity issues, not just those related to tracking, but to reports surrounding retention, disciplinary actions, academic deficiency and dropouts.

Closely related to the issue of tracking and so often leading to similar outcomes is a language of judgment, almost exclusively normative in nature, which has become rather commonplace in the schools. Children and young people are invariably and unfortunately tied to one or more labels. The one thing we know for certain about these labels, whether positive or negative in a literal sense, is that they tend to limit an individual's possibilities because they often circumscribe what we see and expect. And as we have come increasingly to understand, expectations mean close to everything. In addition, the labels are almost always poorly connected to the whole of a person.

A way to change much that goes on in a school is to help alter the ways children and young people are discussed, described, and written about. Ensuring that students' learning is noted in many diverse settings and in relation to a variety of learning activities would help. This, of course, would demand that teachers share their knowledge of students. Beginning all focused discussions relating to students with a description of their strengths is another means. When strengths are the starting point, the language changes and the learning possibilities grow. Considering ways to keep our discourse focused on strengths is also related closely to empowerment.

I need, obviously, to bring this to an end, even though each vignette I have discussed caused me to think of at least five more with equal power. My purpose has been to share a perspective on teachers growing in their profession, becoming increasingly "students of teaching." Without the authoritativeness growing out of sound knowledge, control of the language, and an openness to group thought—qualities teachers have the capacity for gaining in large measure, and the basis of what I have chosen to call teacher empowerment—schools are not likely to get much better.

Nine

Refining the
Craft of Teaching

This discussion is intended as a companion to the previous chapter on teacher empowerment. Taking the same basic theme, it describes activities that can enlarge your understandings of practice and through which you can gain fuller control of a more inspiring and generative language of teaching and learning. In this regard, it is more about becoming the "students of teaching" that the schools need.

In the early 1970s, more than a hundred North Dakota teachers and I, along with several other University of North Dakota faculty members, engaged ourselves in focused conversations around John Dewey's formulation of "becoming students of teaching." This work serves as a base for this chapter. Even though it is a twenty-year-old experience, it fits well many current interests. Among the products of this activity, which I will describe more fully later, were a *Teacher Interview* (Center for Teaching and Learning, 1972) and a *Staff Development Handbook* (Center for Teaching and Learning, 1975), which were used extensively in North Dakota and in many other parts of the United States. The interview and the handbook, while long out of print, still get enthusiastic responses from teachers, who see in them many renewing possibilities.

I can't describe easily the long days we talked together about what it meant to be a student of teaching. The summer seminars at

the University of North Dakota, where we read a variety of philosophical essays and books, shared our various understandings with
each other, and engaged in collective exercises oriented toward
"staff development," were particularly intensive. The decision making around the handbook and the teacher discussion groups that
formed and met regularly in many different communities around
the state were particularly inspiring to me. A powerful community
of teachers emerged, made up of individuals who came to understand well the critical nature of their work as they became increasingly more authoritative about their practice. The control they
gained over their teaching craft was remarkable.

The friendships that developed among us in those years en-
dure. One of the teachers in this group, a person with a good ear
for children's language, called me recently because she knew I
would want to hear some interesting conceptual language from
children in her kindergarten class who were discussing the "growing of rocks." She was right: the dialogue she recounted was indeed
delightful, particularly because it was so rich in detail. Many of the
other teachers from those years also keep me up-to-date on their
work, continuing, it is clear, to be careful observers of children who
reflect deeply on their practice.

So much for background. Now I will move directly to some
of the literature and ideas that provided a context for our work
together.

Seymour Sarason, in his *Culture of the Schools and the Problem of Change* ([1973] 1982), a book I recommend, notes that
teachers, after five years, "felt as competent as they ever were to feel
and they verbalized no expectations that they would be teaching or
thinking differently in the future . . . these teachers indicated that
they rarely experienced any more a sense of personal and intellectual growth. The shape of the future was quite clear . . . a routine
with which they were already quite familiar" (pp. 163–164). While
most of us, I suspect, might acknowledge that such conclusions
have some foundation, especially at a time when so much is being
mandated from sources beyond individual schools, we need also to
resist them. Most teachers I know desire much more from their
professional lives and if provided reasonable opportunities and pro-

fessional support would maintain their enthusiasm for teaching and continue to be productive learners.

Given the conditions that exist in many of our schools and the limited support teachers receive in many communities, it is actually surprising that so many *have* survived as learners, growing personally and professionally. But their continued growth and sense of optimism are more often a tribute to their individual initiative and perseverance than to any particular design of a school system, colleges and universities, or state educational agencies.

Some school administrators protest such a belief, suggesting that inservice education is an item of high priority in *their* districts. And colleges and universities, as well as state education agencies, may also feel that they have creative inservice programs for teachers. Good intentions abound, and often stimulating programs are presented. But even when well done, the capacity of most large-scale inservice education activities to cause teachers to alter in any significant manner the nature of their classroom practices or their knowledge of ways to extend children's learning or their own is relatively small.

Largely this is because most inservice activities are too general. They are typically organized externally by school administrators, colleges and universities, state education agencies, or districtwide teacher committees around learning activities *they* believe teachers (as a general population within a particular district or school) need. The needs are often determined by a desire to introduce, for example, a new curriculum or a new reading series. In some school districts, however, inservice activities are based on "needs assessment" data gathered from large numbers of teachers. My experience with this latter process is that the specific needs and interests provided by an *individual* teacher ("I would like assistance in getting my second-graders into writing") assume very broad, more general form when they are summarized at a central office ("Teachers say they want assistance in language arts"). The result is that *few* teachers receive in the resulting inservice workshops precisely what they identified as being important to them.

More positive inservice and staff development directions, organized and developed by teachers themselves, are possible and could bring about for many teachers renewed enthusiasm for learning and renewed confidence in their capacity to make educational decisions. Before suggesting some of these directions for stimulating teacher growth, at least two assumptions (drawn in part from Bussis, Chittenden, and Amarel, 1976) need to be established: first, that the quality of teachers' understandings influences to a large degree what teachers do in the classroom; second, that the best source for teachers to learn more about teaching and learning, growth and development of children, materials and methods, is through an examination of their own practice and their own classrooms.

Maxine Greene in *The Teacher as Stranger: Educational Philosophy for the Modern Age* (1973) provides a clear extension of those assumptions: "Teaching is purposeful action . . . [the teacher's] intentions will inevitably be affected by the assumptions he makes regarding human nature and human possibility. Many of these assumptions are hidden; most have never been activated. If he is to achieve clarity and full consciousness, the teacher must attempt to make such assumptions explicit; for only then can they be examined, analyzed and understood" (pp. 69–70).

I have come to understand, more now than ever before, that teachers have not had many opportunities, nor have they been encouraged, to systematically examine their purposes and practices. Such an understanding was affirmed in the early 1970s through the use of our *Teacher Interview,* a structured, open-ended protocol that provides a context for individual teachers to reflect on their intentions, use of materials, relationships with children, and organization of time and space, as well as perceptions of difficulties and successes. I have used the teacher interviews again in recent years, experiencing similar responses.

The interview was designed initially as a program evaluation instrument, but it rather quickly became a useful staff development tool. Teachers then as now have described the interview experience as one of their most intense and revealing inservice activities.

The interview (two to four hours long) causes teachers to consider, among other things, why they organize their classroom as they do, why they use specific materials as opposed to other materials, why they pursue particular goals and not other goals. It has stimulated many teachers to articulate educational directions they want to pursue and has encouraged them to organize the necessary resources to go forward. I have provided below a small sample of the questions and probes in the interview (see Exhibit 1). You will probably think of many others that can help you and colleagues get more deeply into the interior of your practices.

The interview activity tended to foster a variety of documentation practices. This was especially true in the early 1970s, when the project I am using as the base for this discussion had so much support built into it. Some teachers began to keep daily journals in which they noted particularly important occurrences, positive and negative responses of children, peer interaction, children's use of various materials, and questions asked by children. Others began to document specific aspects of their instructional programs—reading, writing, the creative arts.

Exhibit 1. Sample Teacher Interview Questions.

	Question	*Probes*
1.	Let's begin with a description of your classroom. As a stranger, what would I see if I walked into your room? How is the room arranged or organized?	a. What would I see as I looked around the room at the walls? b. How is the furniture arranged? c. Where is your desk? d. What kinds of books, resource materials, construction materials are there? e. Where do they come from? f. How often are they used?
1a.	Has the arrangement of the room or the kinds of materials present changed any over the course of the year? How has it changed?	a. How did these changes come about?
2.	We know that no two days are alike, but we'd like to get a general picture of what a typical teaching day (or class) is like. Would you describe for me how a day (or class) is organized?	a. When would you usually do that? b. How long would that usually last? c. Are there specific times scheduled for particular activities? When? d. Why have you organized in that way? What other possibilities have you considered?
3.	Let's change our focus now. Could you discuss the sorts of things that you want your students to learn? In other words, what areas of learning are most important to you as a teacher?	

Exhibit 1. Sample Teacher Interview Questions, Cont'd.

Question	Probes
3a. Okay, you mentioned [*list the areas of importance mentioned*]. Now, let's talk about how you try to accomplish these in terms of specific activities, materials, questions. Let's start with [*select one of the areas mentioned*]. What sorts of things do your students do in _____ ? [*This can be followed by a second or third.*]	a. How do these activities get started? b. How are the students organized during these activities? If I came in while that was going on what would I see? Would the students be working alone, in small groups, or all together as a class? c. How many would be involved in these activities? d. What would others be doing during that time? e. How often would these activities go on in the classroom, or how often has that happened? f. What would you be doing while these activities were going on? g. What materials or resources are used during these activities? h. Where do these materials or resources come from? i. How do you evaluate progress in these activities? What would cause you to say that the students have enlarged their understandings?
4. Do you find ways of integrating the learning activities in your classroom? (For example: reading activities with science, history with literature.)	a. Can you describe the way that happens? b. How often does that happen? c. Does it occur in other areas as well?
4a. How has the integration of learning activities changed over the course of the year?	a. Why has there been change? b. How do you feel about that?
9b. What roles do you feel competition and cooperation should play in the classroom?	a. Do you find the words "competition" and "cooperation" useful in describing children's behavior and classroom interaction? b. Can you describe activities in your room which promote competition? Which promote cooperation? c. How do you feel about the role competition and cooperation play in your classroom?

Exhibit 1. Sample Teacher Interview Questions, Cont'd.

Question	Probes
14. Now, we'd like you to reflect upon opportunities you may have to talk about important aspects of your teaching experience with others. For example, with teachers in your building, with your principal, or others at conferences or meetings. [*Pause.*] Are there persons you try out your ideas on; ask for help; share both your doubts and failures as well as your aspirations and accomplishments as a teacher? Could you give some examples?	a. How valuable are these opportunities to you? b. Do you wish there were more opportunities to talk with others about your teaching? c. How could this be made to happen more often? d. In general, do you feel that the kind of things you are trying to do in your classroom is understood and supported in your school?

We'd like to shift our focus now to think about the growth of individual children in your classroom. Could you select the tenth child in your class list. Think about that person for a moment. Now, could you tell me something about him or her?

22. How would you assess the quality of his or her learning?

22a. How would you characterize the quality of his or her thinking? (Examples?)

22b. What kinds of questions does he or she raise in the classroom? (Examples?)

22c. Does he or she select projects and activities that challenge him or her to think? (Examples?)

22d. What does he or she seem to value highly? What are his or her strongly held beliefs? Does he or she seem aware of those values, beliefs?

22e. How does he or she interact with others?

22f. How does he or she react to rules?

The following account comes from one teacher's efforts to document aspects of his practice (Perrone, 1977b).

I began by observing various activities in my classroom for short periods of time each day. I made anecdotal records of my observations in a notebook. The results were not astounding but the entries helped me to confirm many of the notions I had and also raised some questions.

After making many broad observations . . . I decided to investigate . . . math because that subject was least appealing to the children. I began observing and recording both my activities and the children's . . . my observations indicated an inconsistency be-

tween my philosophy and my practice. In spite of my
strong belief that manipulative math experiences help
children to understand math concepts, I was doing
little in the way of teaching with these materials
or encouraging their use in independent study. . . .
[Some new directions were begun.] Since my first attempt as a teacher-researcher, I have continued to experiment with alternative manipulative experiences in
math, using a variety of settings and levels. Through
careful observation and recording, I have come to
more specific conclusions about the purpose and use
of manipulative experiences. Using the same process
during the past five years I have become involved in
research on lab approaches to social studies and science,
vocabulary development, language experience, parent-
child-teacher conferences, values clarification, multi-
age grouping, parent meetings [p. 4].

The kinds of documentation activities implied in that account have assisted many teachers in their classroom-based reflections. And in many settings teachers pursuing such documentation
activities began to come together to share their insights with each
other, to discuss education as "students of teaching." This collective
work was particularly constructive.

We began very early to use the "teacher as researcher" notion
as a way to describe the documentation activities. It was a particularly useful way of giving credence to the ways teachers were beginning to examine their work. The conception of teacher research
that is currently in vogue typically denotes a researcher-teacher collaboration. While acknowledging then that such a formulation
could be constructive, we saw the teacher research directions within
our project as a critical precursor to this recent method, helping
teachers gain greater independence and more co-equal status with
external researchers from the colleges and universities.

In regard to teacher research, Ann Cook and Herb Mack ask
in *The Word and the Thing: Ways of Seeing the Teacher* (1974),
"Are teachers becoming more self-reliant, able to determine not
only what to do with children but why to do it? Are they able to

evaluate the degree of their success in a particular subject or with a specific child?" (p. 7). Many of the teachers who participated in the teacher interview and subsequent documentation activities could certainly have answered yes to such a question. They traveled far toward becoming thoughtful, analytical, independent professionals relying on their own initiative and critical judgment.

Approximately thirty of the teachers who had been involved in the teacher interviews and the early documentation activities came together in the summer of 1974 to discuss their reflective efforts. They became the core group responsible for developing a *Staff Development Handbook*. The handbook was designed to assist other classroom teachers in organizing their *own* efforts to become students of teaching.

Their initial draft was subsequently reviewed by several hundred North Dakota teachers and, over a year's time, the handbook went through at least eight different revisions. The final product was, I believe, an exemplary sample of what teachers can do when provided an opportunity to act as professionals.

It is hardly possible here to share the handbook in its entirety; yet I believe that a sample of its contents might be useful. The basic organizational construct of the handbook reflected the growth of the teachers who worked on it; fittingly, they used components of growth as their framework. The components and some operational definitions are shown as Exhibit 2.

Exhibit 2. Components of Growth, Teacher Handbook.

Awareness/Reflection

Beginning to wonder, to question, to search, to step back and view ourselves as we actually are.

- What are my strengths as a teacher?
- What do I know about how children learn?
- How do my beliefs and attitudes about teaching guide the decisions I make about my classroom practice?

Trust

Feeling safe enough to experiment, discuss, admit problems, fail, ask questions, seek help, maintain faith in ourselves and others. Trust develops in an atmosphere where you are known for what you are, understood

Exhibit 2. Components of Growth, Teacher Handbook, Cont'd.

for where you've been, accepted for whom you've become, and *still* are gently invited to grow.

- Where can I find support as I reflect upon the uncertainties and questions I have about my teaching?
- Are there others with whom I can share ideas, questions and concerns?

Opportunities for Growth

Being able to recognize the value of new experiences, to create opportunities for growth where they do not seem to exist.

- Who are the people who can assist me to grow personally and professionally?
- How can I arrange my day so that I will have time to seek out opportunities for growth?

Risk

Gambling that you'll be successful in an attempt to work with children in a different manner. It is taking a chance and leaving yourself open to failure.

- How do I develop a sufficient level of confidence to take some risks?
- Why is it so difficult to begin new patterns of doing things?

Working Plans

Implementing one's beliefs and intentions about teaching and learning; reflecting about the needs of individual children; organizing materials which support children's learning.

- How can I put into practice what I believe about children's learning?
- What kind of relationship do I want with children? How should I organize the classroom? How should time be organized? What kinds of materials should be available?
- How can I divide my really big ideas into parts that are small enough so that I dare to make a beginning? Whom can I talk with about my ideas?

Conflict

Experiencing personal uneasiness and anxiety when dealing with risk taking. Finding the internal and external resources and strength to resolve puzzling questions and apprehensions.

- How can I know that my teaching practice is really assisting children with their learning?
- How can I respond to the many questions and concerns of my colleagues as well as the parents of children with whom I work?

For each of these six components, a series of theoretical-philosophical statements and corresponding practical suggestions was developed. The intention of using both was to create a dialectical exchange. A small sample of the suggestions (without the philosophical statements) appears as Exhibit 3. They are taken from sections of the handbook relating to awareness and reflection, opportunities for growth, and working plans.

Exhibit 3. Sample Suggestions, Teacher Handbook.

Awareness and Reflection

Think about and write down five learning experiences of your own you can recall.

> Why was it important?
> In what setting did it occur?
> Were others involved in the experience?
> Was there anything special about what you learned?
> Was there anything unique about you at that time?
> Draw generalizations about the conditions under which you learn best.
> Share your learnings with someone else.
> Does this help you to look differently at the way children in your classroom learn?

Deliberately and systematically reflect on your classroom practice.

- Take 15 minutes at the close of your morning (or day) and write all the important things you can think of that happened in your classroom. Notice how much more observant you become after a week or two.
- Use the questions on the teacher interview to examine and clarify your classroom experiences.
    - —Describe your classroom. How is it arranged and organized? Why do you have it this way?
    - —In your classroom, how are children involved in making decisions about their learning?
    - —In your classroom, what happens when a rule isn't followed?
- Observe some element of your classroom over a long period of time (peer interaction). Keep a log of your observations.
- Document carefully some aspect of your program; for example, reading or creative arts.
    - —Write a statment of purposes.
    - —Keep logs on daily activities.
    - —Maintain samples of children's work.

Opportunities for Growth

Survey your real interests, the things you do outside of school. Take one of your personal interests into your classroom tomorrow.

Exhibit 3. Sample Suggestions, Teacher Handbook, Cont'd.

Organize staff development and teacher growth groups in your school.

- A small group of teachers and principals get together and discuss particular children and their learning every Thursday afternoon.

Use the teacher interview as a tool for reflection and personal evaluation.

- Use questions from the interview with one other person.
- Use questions from the interview as a base for discussion.

Do action research and documentation in your classroom in order to clarify what you do in the classroom and explore its effects on children.

- Take note of a specific part of your classroom experience over a period of time (or invite someone else to observe this element on a regular basis).
  —A student who puzzles you.
  —The way students spend their time, the choices they make, the effect or results of a particular teaching method, the kinds of questions students ask.
- Collect data related to a concern you have.
  Samples of a student's writing over a period of time.
  Samples of children's artwork.
  Videotape or tape record your class in action.

Working Plans

Use the community as a resource.

- Invite local people to explain their work, the tools they use, how they spend their day, what sorts of things they do when they're not working.
- Visit a variety of community resources.
- Plan with a business for children to spend an extended time with them (maybe a week)—a sort of short-term apprentice program.

Plan and implement a different evaluation and reporting system.

- Keep anecdotal records of children's classroom activities, behavior, interactions with other people.
- Regularly collect samples of children's work.
- Use narrative reporting and frequent formal and informal conferencing with parents and their children.
- Hold as many parent conferences as possible in the classroom during the school day while the children are working.
- Meet with parents and children in their homes.

These suggestions are by no means all-inclusive but they should provide a flavor of the handbook and its basic orientation. None of us who worked on it suggested that it should serve as *the* basis for a staff development effort for which individuals and groups of teachers might take responsibility. Growth, after all, is a highly personal process, which occurs as individuals find ways to reflect, as well as act, on their experiences. But the handbook does represent a starting point for growth; in addition, and this I believe is significant, it attempts to encourage teachers to rely more on their own personal resources and those of their colleagues.

You might want to work with some of the ideas. You might also share with colleagues what you learned. And over time you and your teaching colleagues might well become the thoughtful teachers you most wish to be. In the end, the schools will get better as teachers themselves become students of teaching, able to assume the principal responsibility for all aspects of teaching and learning.

Ten

The Next Generation
of Teachers

As teachers we need to be concerned about the ongoing recruitment and preparation of *new* teachers. We shouldn't leave this entirely to public officials, the marketplace, or the schools of education. While many fields of endeavor are important, few match the significance of teaching, with its social and moral obligations to support the intellectual and community-oriented growth of children and young people.

Currently, interest in teaching is enlarging rapidly. In large measure, this is a response to the expanding demand for teachers alongside a higher than usual level of public support for the importance of education. But it also has a lot to do with a resurgence of idealism and social commitment among many of our young people.

The last time conditions were similar—the 1950s and most of the 1960s—traditional standards for new teachers tended to be put aside. At the time, many felt this merely filled the schools with large numbers of "warm bodies," but the basic argument was unfair. I found the "warm bodies" discussion discouraging because it diminished the commitments and idealism of most of those who entered teaching. I also thought the negative discourse dampened enthusiasm for the creative approaches to the preparation of teachers and different ways of conceptualizing schools that were developing in these years.

110

This time around, in spite of the massive shortages of teachers being predicted for the last decade of the twentieth century, efforts are being made to *increase* preparation demands and standards rather than relax them. While alternative certification programs are currently receiving considerable public attention, possibly suggesting a lessening of standards, they are small efforts with only minor effect on the larger discussion of teacher education.

Contemporary efforts to bring about teacher education reform are being led principally by the Holmes Group, which is a university-based movement, and the Carnegie Forum on Education and the Economy, which developed a broad constituency involving teachers, school administrators, teacher unions, political and governmental leaders, and representatives from business and industry. Both have had a measure of success in encouraging colleges and universities to reconceptualize their teacher education programs and state departments of education to reconstruct their certification requirements.

The agenda of the Holmes Group, and to some degree the Carnegie Forum, calls essentially for teachers to complete liberal arts programs, followed by year-long internships in settings that are supportive of teacher professionalism—schools where teachers are active curriculum makers and have important roles in shaping the teaching and learning environments. There is also an expectation that the internship (clinical or professional development) schools will be closely connected to colleges and universities and their intellectual and practice-oriented resources.

Both reform groups stress the need to recruit intellectually able, resourceful, socially committed people. This suggests, in their terms, "high standards" for entry into teaching as evidenced by good college grades, passing a variety of subject matter and basic skills examinations, and demonstrating professional competence through performance reviews in clinical practice settings. Beyond these entry-level requirements, the Carnegie Forum has encouraged through a National Board for Professional Teaching, a voluntary national certification process involving portfolios of accomplishment and work samples and a series of formal performance-oriented assessments. Analogous to the national board examinations for medical practitioners, this process will, it is hoped, raise the stature of the teaching profession and provide a credible means for the differentiation of teachers.

An underlying belief of these reform directions is that this higher level of preparation will foster additional public support for teachers, causing teacher salaries and status to increase, thus attracting more academically able men and women. I believe most of the directions being proposed are useful, but I don't anticipate events will necessarily follow the linear path being suggested. Because teaching is principally a public enterprise dependent on tax revenues, expecting teachers' salaries to match those in such fields as law, medicine, engineering, or commerce is unrealistic. Of course, salary considerations are important, and salary levels do need to grow, but the people that schools most need are people for whom money is not the *primary* concern, the reason they choose teaching rather than law. Also, the complexities of evaluation, whether at the level of initial certification or beyond, will certainly continue to create problems, in part because teaching is so situation-bound and filled with so many uncertainties. As a human activity overflowing with idiosyncratic qualities, teaching will always have a host of rough edges. Under the circumstances, the search for one, even two, best solutions to the preparation of new teachers and the retention of experienced teachers is quixotic. We will surely be better served by multiple reform directions, many more than those currently being advocated.

Aside from these major directions of teacher education reform, there is much that current teachers can do in their own classrooms and schools to foster a new generation of thoughtful teachers. In the end, the work of teachers will be more important in this recruitment arena than most of what currently passes for teacher education reform.

On the recruitment side, teachers can make their largest contributions through the examples they provide to their own students, day in and day out. After all, future generations of teachers are sitting with teachers each day in hundreds of thousands of classrooms across the country. Through the enthusiasm teachers project in their work and the encouragement they give to those who express interest in teaching, teachers can play a particularly important role in ensuring an ongoing supply of teachers for subsequent generations of students.

Knowing this, it might be useful to reflect on the images of teaching we project and the ways we talk about teaching with our students. Do students see us enjoying what we do? Do we share with them how socially useful teaching can be, the opportunities it provides for continuing to be learners? Do we share our hopes and our efforts for more favorable working conditions? Do we provide an understanding that conditions can and need to be better? That schools can and need to be better? Do we place our work in schools within an understandable historical framework as well as the contemporary social context? Or, do we focus most heavily on our martyrdom? Our unhappiness? Our wish to be doing something else?

A recent (1989) survey of sophomore students in secondary schools conducted by the Southeastern Educational Laboratory found that only 5.8 percent expressed any interest in teaching as a career (*Education Daily*, 1989). This won't come close to what the schools are projected to require in the next decade. And most of the 5.8 percent were white females performing in school at an average level. Students who expressed no interest in becoming teachers—close to 95 percent—noted, in particular, the stress they observed among their own teachers. They also commented on low pay, lack of authority, and poor working conditions.

I hear teachers in many settings speak constantly about the negative aspects of their work. They say to students, "You'd have to be crazy to go into teaching." This message apparently gets through to their own children, as fewer than 2 percent in the foregoing survey said they would consider teaching.

Beyond the example provided to their own students, teachers can also assume in even larger ways an important role in the preparation of new teachers. Traditionally, teacher involvement has meant supervising student teachers (as cooperating teachers or practitioners). This takes time, and it means giving up some control of a classroom, but teachers need to continue this critical activity, viewing it as a professional responsibility and a source of ongoing professional enrichment. It is becoming increasingly more difficult to find thoughtful teachers willing to work regularly with student teachers and interns.

A healthy way of thinking about the student teaching or intern experience is to consider it in team-teaching, collegial terms, as an opportunity to share ideas, students, and curriculum, and as a means of providing *more* support for students' learning. Of course we must take into account where these new teachers are in their professional development and levels of confidence. They will not know everything we might think they should know. But weren't we, at a parallel time in our lives, in much the same place? There must be a full legion of now-retired cooperating teachers who shook their heads often about all we didn't know back then. The skills, knowledge, and understandings we veteran teachers possess about teaching and learning in school settings have clearly come from an accumulation of experience, something we occasionally tend to forget. These student teachers will join us soon enough in similar skills, knowledge, and understandings. Our hope must be, of course, that they will come to be even more effective than we have been.

Typically, these new teachers enter our schools with considerable idealism. They often see in teaching the fulfillment of a social service commitment. They talk about "democracy" and "responsibility" and the need to bring an "intellectual character" to their work. We should encourage such idealism rather than diminish its value with talk about the "real world" or claims that "schools can't be like that." If our own sense of idealism is waning, we might be buoyed by the enthusiasm of our student teachers and interns. Idealism needs support. We need to remember that idealism is an important lifeline to a teaching life filled with possibilities.

Also for the practicum experience to be optimal, these new teachers need cooperating teachers who encourage them to make use of units, themes, approaches that they themselves understand and feel will work (rather than mirroring primarily *our* ways of engaging students). We need to refrain from suggesting too often, "I tried that once and it didn't work."

These student teachers also need cooperating teachers willing to share their own understandings of teaching, their own aspirations for their students; to discuss why they do what they do in the classroom rather than something else, use a particular set of materials and not others, organize this way and not in other ways; and to interact about pedagogical and content issues, philosophically as well as practically. In other words, they need access to cooperating teachers' assumptions about teaching and learning along with their decision-making processes. This more scholarly side of the experienced teacher's work must stand out as an example to new teachers. John Dewey wrote of the need for teachers to be "students of teaching," the base for his "teacher as scholar" conception. It is a posture we should strive to achieve in our work. Having a student teacher can enhance such a direction.

In addition, experienced teachers need to be willing to serve as mentors for first- and second-year teachers. These are critical years. Many potentially excellent teachers lose their interest in teaching at this early point and are lost to the profession. Many could have been retained with ongoing support and encouragement. In the early weeks, mentors will likely be involved in a variety of security-building activities—helping the beginning teachers to meet others, get to know the setting, figure out the ongoing protocols of attendance and records, and organize their classroom space. But these practical needs will end soon enough, and the more sustaining issues of professionalism, if nurtured, will grow in importance. Mentors can begin to read with the new teachers, provide opportunities for them to reflect systematically on their practice, and make sure they observe in a variety of classroom settings, not just to see other teachers at work, but to see as well many of their own students in different environments. This is particularly valuable to new teachers as a way of helping them understand their students more fully, being in a position to support more constructively their growth.

When young teachers ask me about preparation activities, I suggest they learn to be careful observers of children and young people in the natural·environment, watching them in the subways, trains, and buses, in the streets, at parks and playgrounds, listening to them talk with each other and with others, getting a larger view of the similar as well as different patterns. Teaching, after all, is about *knowing* children well. Seeing them outside of a school setting is particularly important. What we often learn is that children and young people are competent, imaginative, able to be attentive to conversation and what is around them, and tend to be responsible. Given the structures in many of our schools, it is quite easy to see many of these youngsters as having few of these qualities.

There is, of course, a strong imperative for the schools themselves to be centers for inquiry. If schools are to be places that encourage new teachers, causing them to see teaching as an interesting and unique career, they have to be intellectually and socially challenging environments in which teachers read together, reflect on practice, develop curriculum with a local, situated quality, and become conscious about the development of a learning community. What better way to encourage new teachers—and also sustain the enthusiasm of experienced teachers.

In the process of building a fully generative learning community, it is often constructive for schools to be reciprocally engaged in a collaboration with colleges and universities. Given their traditions of reflection and scholarship, colleges and universities can contribute to schools becoming the professionally rich and educationally stimulating environments they need to be if the well-being of their faculties is to thrive, if young people and their communities are to be well served, and if a new generation of teachers is to be well prepared. The collaboration can also have an impact on the college or university. There is, for example, no reason why experienced teachers could not be collaborators in most college courses related to teacher education. They could help translate academic content into teachable material and constructs, initiate students into curriculum development, and share their experience. Their presence would make the university experience more engaging. The current movement to create professional development schools that link preservice and inservice education is intended to support these kinds of partnership activities. In most settings, however, they haven't reached a very high level of reciprocity. The colleges and universities are too dominant.

Teachers are seldom asked what they believe makes for the best preparation. And when they are asked, the questions are confined to concerns about courses, techniques, and the length of the clinical practice. Such questions encourage *technical* responses about such matters as lesson plans, attendance, record books, academic majors and minors. But when given opportunities to talk about their own work, what makes it captivating, what from their collegiate background and ongoing reflection contributes most to their successful practice, the technical pieces fade and the conversation changes. The issues become more complex, not as linear as teacher education programs in colleges and universities typically are, not easily reduced to a course on this or that. The solution has more to do with predispositions toward inquiry and reflection, curiosity, a particular intellectual passion, a social commitment, a set of beliefs, a love for the unexpected, a general interest in human growth and development.

The exceptional teachers I know are passionate about learning. They have deep interests in some aspect of learning—history, literature, science. They are so steeped in this passion that they could manage well if all the textbooks, workbooks, and curricular guides that fill the schools suddenly disappeared. They see connecting points everywhere. It is not possible to take a walk with them without noting that they are almost always seeing around them possibilities for their students. They make particular note of books, insist on "checking out" libraries and museums, write down addresses of people and places. Schools need to promote and support passion of this kind. Teachers need opportunities to reflect on their learning, on how they first came to the interests they possess and how to revitalize those interests. This suggests once more the need for schools to be settings where teachers share their learning with each other, read together, and have opportunities for writing and further study. The school needs to be a center of inquiry, an intellectually oriented place.

Teachers can also contribute to the improvement of teacher education by producing a more uplifting literature about teaching. This brings me back to the teacher-as-scholar theme. We need a richer literature written by classroom teachers who work in settings where teaching continues to have potency. Such a literature would provide a counterbalance to the descriptions of teachers as managers, passing out and collecting worksheets which are geared to skill deficiencies identified by scores on a host of standardized and criterion referenced tests. It would also get us beyond many of the current definitions of effective teaching, especially in settings with a predominance of minority and poor children—namely, carefully sequenced curriculum, whole-group instruction, drill, a narrow range of materials, little elaboration, and questions of a low cognitive nature.

It would be helpful, in this regard, if teachers reflected more and wrote more about what is important in their teaching and what has sustained them, using these reflections to offer suggestions about the preparation and support of new teachers. One particularly thoughtful effort of this kind is presented in *Speaking Out: Teachers and Teaching* (Traugh and others, 1986).

There is a good deal of conversation today about where teacher preparation should occur. Certainly more of it should take place *in the schools* and teachers need to be central to that. Colleges and universities, however, need also to be deeply involved. But does that mean all colleges and universities, or just some? I am not prepared to argue, as many do, that teacher education should be limited to big research-oriented and traditional liberal arts colleges and universities. Such a view is certainly not very helpful to many of the historically black institutions that have long been the principal source of black teachers. And it limits the overall pool by closing off some of the only institutions accessible to many other individuals. At the same time, I still want to make sure, as all teachers should, that our highest-status institutions (Harvard, Yale, Stanford, the University of Michigan, the University of California, Berkeley, among others) see the preparation of teachers as a critical dimension of their work. If teacher preparation is not a priority at these kinds of institutions, teaching will not be the status field it needs to be.

In thinking about new teachers, one last point might be useful. There is, at the moment, a good deal of talk about the restructuring of schools, and I expect constructive activity in the years ahead. As we move in some different directions, I would hope that those in schools might bring greater imagination to staffing. Full-time teachers are, of course, essential. Schools and the students they serve need the regularities, the continuities that full-time teachers provide. But schools also need as many diverse individuals as possible, those with a variety of specialized skills, interests, and experiences. Many of these could be part time: medical practitioners, dancers, actors, painters, sculptors, musicians, writers, artisans. Such persons can enrich a school intellectually and culturally, making it an even more interesting and sustaining setting.

In this period of renewal, teachers themselves need to assume a larger responsibility for ensuring that teaching becomes an intentional professional field capable of attracting a steady supply of highly qualified new members. This chapter is intended to outline some of the current circumstances and establish some constructive directions now and for the future.

Eleven

The Importance of
Historical Perspective

We work in a field that has a very long history. This may be obvious, but that history is not something we think about enough, make a part of our ongoing reflections about teaching, learning, and schools. At one level, if we are not well connected to our educational history, we can lose sight of the dignity of teaching and its larger social context. We need to know that committed men and women over many hundreds of years have seen in teaching the opportunity to build a safer, more humane, and economically productive world. Their stories, the ways they conceptualized their work, help connect us across time and place, enlarging our understanding of the roots of our work and providing us considerable personal and professional inspiration.

An another level, the lack of historical perspective leads us to interpret too much of what passes for reform—change in schools—as new when, in fact, much of the reform had an earlier history. It prevents us, as well, from learning from the previous history of reform. If, for example, we made a practice of reading older descriptions of school reform, learning about the ways school curricula, organizational structures, and instructional practices were affected, as well as the political, economic, and social factors that influenced them, we might have a better grasp of what educational reform demands, not only in historical terms but presently.

Much of the 1960s educational reform could have profited from a more significant connection to the earlier progressive literature and the reform movement that surrounded progressivism, particularly in relation to curriculum. It was surprising, for example, how obscure John Dewey's work was to so many 1960s educators.

A particularly critical value, for me, in staying close to the historical literature as I work with teachers to improve, even reconstruct, the schools that now exist, is understanding the shifting patterns of language that surround our work. It is valuable to know that the definitions that now prevail in critical educational constructs—vocational education, excellence, learning, time, memory—had at other times richer meanings, laden with larger possibilities. Because many of the words themselves have remained the same, there is a semblance of continuity when, in fact, the discontinuities are overwhelming.

When John Dewey spoke of vocations and work, for example, he was concerned about the development of constructive attitudes about the *value* of work, the need for children and young people to appreciate accomplishment borne of sustained effort, to attach personal meaning to their intellectual inquiries and practical activities. And given his understandings of the changes in the economic order, he wanted students to comprehend the complexities of an industrial age. But in relation to the economic system, he *did not* view vocational education in the schools as a means of preparing workers for American industry. And significantly considering how vocational education has developed, Dewey never envisioned vocational study separated from academic study, a separate track for those judged intellectually inadequate.

Further, when Dewey wrote about memory in relation to thinking, he wasn't discussing recall, the recitation of isolated facts. Memory was a larger construction, the fitting together of many images, many conceptions, something whole, and always in relation to the establishment of extended meaning. Moreover, the importance he attached to community studies and democratic participation meant more than walks to the fire station and the passive student councils that fill the schools.

Dewey is not the subject of this chapter. But in the spirit of this discussion on historical perspective, I want to provide a personal synthesis of his educational thought that helps me consider more fully my current work in and around schools, even as I recognize that such a reduction can't do justice to his original ideas. For this, we would all do well to reread, in particular, *The School and Society* (Dewey, [1989] 1956), *The Child and the Curriculum* (Dewey, [1902] 1956), *How We Think* (Dewey, 1910), *Democracy and Education* (Dewey, [1916] 1961), and *Experience and Education* (Dewey, [1938] 1963). Needless to say, I find Dewey particularly provocative as we turn increasingly to a belief that the schools need to change. His thought should be much more common in our contemporary educational discourse. Here is my beginning synthesis:

- Education and life are part of the same social continuity—not separate pieces.
- Education is growth.
- Continuity of experience is basic to growth, the thread that brings about consolidation of ideas, and their meanings.
- Experience is the basis for all genuine education—even though all experiences are not equally educative.
- The interests of children and the adult interest in curriculum are reciprocal.
- The development of intelligence and knowledge, whether for an individual or a culture, grows from cooperative exchange.
- The most effective learning comes from doing, acting on the world.

Dewey saw skills such as reading, writing, and arithmetic as understandings derived from needs growing out of activities, not as skills to be taught apart from natural inquiry. We should revive that perspective in schools, especially as reading, writing, and arithmetic have become increasingly disconnected from any significant intellectual content. It is discouraging to see so much of children's education revolve around workbook exercises and simple text, materials that have meaning *only* in school, that are so unrelated to our larger cultural heritage.

A lack of historical perspective is particularly evident in the "reform" era that was set off by *A Nation at Risk* (National Commission on Excellence in Education, 1983). Many of the discussions that occurred around this report called on us to believe that there was a time when *all* students could read and write easily and well, studied foreign languages, completed coursework in physics, possibly calculus, understood political processes at relatively high levels, and were steeped in classical literature and American history. Many in the schools were, unfortunately, put on the defensive by such claims; they themselves came to believe that "the schools *used to be good.*"

We should know, however, that such an implied golden age didn't exist. We didn't even get the majority (51 percent) of students through high school until 1950, and our peak in terms of high school completion—77 percent—was reached just twenty years ago (during the 1960s, no less). As things now stand, we will be hard pressed to reach that level again for many years to come. And even that level is inadequate to today's social and economic needs. Having said that, however, it is discouraging to note in recent surveys of teachers (Carnegie Foundation for the Advancement of Teaching, 1987, 1990) that a significant number *don't* believe it is even realistic to expect more than 75 percent of students to complete high school (graduation rates are now below 71 percent).

Consider foreign languages and physics, supposed exemplars of quality: never in the twentieth century were they studied by more than 25 percent of high school students across the nation. A special reason why "golden" ought not to be a part of our description of the past is that in spite of our longstanding rhetoric of universalism, we have lived for most of our educational history with enormous social, economic, ethnic, and racial inequities, leaving a tragic legacy of broken promises.

I raise all this only to suggest that we would do better not trying to make such qualitative comparisons across time. The generalizations seldom hold up—and they also don't help our children much. They certainly don't need our gratuitous reminders about how poor their education is compared with ours.

There are other features of this current reform movement worthy of examination. The kind of reform being promoted by the current movement—characterized by greater standardization and uniformity through legislative and regulatory action—tends, for example, to coincide historically with periods of economic insecurity and decline in confidence about the future: the early aftermath of the Civil War, the depression years of the 1890s, the pre–World War II Depression years, and the recessionary period of the 1970s (which continues in many respects today).

It is not surprising, within this particular historical formulation, that *A Nation at Risk* focused so heavily on our perceived losses in the economic sphere, building on a belief that we stand in danger of being eclipsed in the international arena, and that its most prominent metaphors were framed around competition and nationalism. It is also not surprising, given the powerful emphasis on loss, to see the previous reform period of the 1960s set off as being at the root of our "current dilemmas" and "fall to mediocrity," even if such charges falter greatly under close examination.

In these periods of reform, which I have characterized as similar to the present reform movement, "returning to basics," "raising standards," and "establishing common requirements" became the dominant definers, the code phrases. Correspondingly, there was a growth in student competency and promotion testing as well as serious concerns about the quality of teachers. That such responses didn't yield particularly positive results earlier seems not to have been considered much in this current wave of reform. Competency tests, or "certifying exams" as they were once called, had, for example, an earlier history. And that history should have taught us about the negative potential—that retention and failure would fall disproportionately on children from minority and poor families and that the tests would come to define the curriculum, narrowing it to minimalist terms.

In contrast to this particular style of reform, which narrowed the boundaries of acceptable practice, providing more technological precision in its definitions, and operating from a premise of scarcity and competition, we have also had reform periods that encouraged considerable diversity in standards and practices, operating from a premise that unlimited possibilities existed. This contrasting direction has generally coincided with periods of economic growth and prosperity and increasing levels of confidence about the future: the Jacksonian democracy years, which extended into the 1840s, the progressive years at the turn of the century, extending somewhat into the 1920s, and the civil rights, socially activist years of the 1960s. These were times when standardization was often seen as debilitating and oppressive, and tightly defined regulations were viewed as obstacles to high-quality education. In these periods, there was more talk about the needs of the child, inquiry-oriented teaching and learning, and equity than about particular curriculum content and learning objectives, direct teaching, and uniformity of standards. Not surprisingly, these were years when teacher education programs attracted particularly able candidates.

As a corollary to this historical review, I want to share one additional observation, which has to do with the involvement of academic scholars in school reform and currently occupies a good deal of my interest. It is another aspect of historical perspective that we should understand.

Academic scholars have, as it turns out, been most involved during the reform periods characterized by more openness, when the definitions were not too precise. A reading of *The Dewey School* (Mayhew and Edwards, [1936] 1966) is fascinating largely because of the work of historians, geographers, and physical scientists. And the materials produced in the 1960s by MIT and Chicago physicists, chemists, and biologists for elementary and secondary school science are exceptional in their inquiry orientation, in contrast to what is being used in most schools today. The same can be said for the history and social science materials produced by historians, economists, anthropologists, and sociologists from Harvard, Carnegie Mellon, Purdue, and the University of California, Berkeley.

The style of the 1960s reform attracted large numbers of academic scholars, not just in materials development but in summer institutes for teachers and inservice education programs, because it focused on inquiry, viewed questions to be more important than answers, understood knowledge to be embedded with more uncertainty than certainty, related more to uncoverage than coverage in regard to curriculum, and considered education to be more humanistic than technological. The current reform movement—characterized as it is by less openness, where learning objectives are framed more narrowly and behaviorally and where a premium is given to information and standardization of curriculum, alongside a more technical language—is alien to much of academic scholarship and has proven less attractive and sustaining. We need ongoing reciprocity between academic scholars and classroom teachers—not the on-again, off-again circumstance that has existed.

I have reviewed these contrasting directions for reform as a means of acknowledging our historically diverse visions about how good education is to be promoted. But in spite of the many reform efforts and regardless of the public rhetoric, I think it's safe to say that the schools themselves, the places where teachers and students actually meet, have generally followed a middle path. They may lean in the particular direction of the reform at hand but seldom do they fully embrace it. As a result, in pedagogical practices and organizational patterns the schools have over time been more the same than truly different. They were, for example, never as child centered as the progressive reform discourse at the turn of the century would suggest, not as curriculum free as the 1960s reform literature might lead us to believe, and not now as rigidly structured, academic, or tough minded as a reading of state regulations might imply. This, too, we should understand. It also needs to be clear, however, that the schools have never been, on a large scale, as good as they should have been, and they are not now.

To speak of historical perspective is also to be attentive to the demographics of schools and communities over time, to understand the nature of the changes. The fact is that schools have become populated, especially in our urban centers, by increasing numbers of nonwhite and non–English-speaking children who are in today's economy living in poverty. As I noted earlier, in twenty-three of the twenty-five largest American cities, the majority of students are from minority backgrounds. Further, one of every five children of school age in our country is poor; in urban communities, where minority populations are particularly large, the figure is closer to one in two.

Given the changing patterns, schools are indeed *different* with regard to the students being served. But we shouldn't let the matter of difference cause us discouragement or resignation. In school after school, veteran administrators and teachers tell me that "the school used to be excellent." (They didn't say, but certainly implied, that the halcyon days were before integration.) At best, they were *different*. They weren't confronting seriously what it means to live in an integrated, more fully democratic, socially just society. That is one of the important challenges of today's schools.

The social context surrounding schools has other historical examples that we should keep before us. We live, as you are aware from the media attention and your own observations, with a child-care crisis as women have entered fully into the labor force and as single parenthood has become so dominant. It is true that only in recent years have women been in the labor market in such large numbers, but women have been working out of the home for many years. Most black mothers, for example, were in the labor market long before "who is caring for the children?" became such a popular question. And in previous periods of heavy immigration, like that we are now going through, whole families were engaged in labor. The point is that there have been other periods when the social service needs of children and families were extensive.

At the turn of the century, Frederick Wirt, superintendent of schools in Gary, Indiana, then a burgeoning industrial town filled with large numbers of immigrants, acknowledged that the schools needed to remain open long after the regular closing hours, on the weekends, and in the summers to ensure children and young people a safe and constructive place to be while their parents worked. The Gary schools became full-blown community schools. And there was an earlier history of schools serving as social service centers—providing breakfast for their students, medical and dental services for children and families, and job training for adults. This was especially true in the 1920s, 1930s, and 1940s. I cite this only to place the controversies about school health clinics and other social service programs in schools in a wider historical context. It isn't only in recent years that schools have assumed these expanding but necessary responsibilities.

In many respects, the limitations in our historical understandings also keep the discussions about the interior of schools much too narrow in scope. The structures, curricular and pedagogical patterns, and relationships with communities that currently exist *appear* to be all there is, possibly all there ever was. Historical perspective would surely enlarge the discourse about what exists. We might come to understand better the circumstances that brought about graded structures and textbooks, Carnegie units and curriculum order, possibly recognizing that such circumstances no longer exist, that what once might have appeared logical and appropriate may no longer be so.

In this vein, James Hernden in *How to Survive in Your Native Land* (1972, pp. 101–102) offers an apocryphal but nonetheless telling story. After describing his work in a junior high school teaching reading to students who lacked much confidence or proficiency in reading, he notes that the students completed their forty-minute period with him, then went for a forty-minute social studies class in "which they got Fs because they couldn't read," then to a forty-minute science class, "where they got Fs because they couldn't read." By the time the school day was over, the students had five or six *F* grades. Wondering why he didn't have the students all day so he could actually teach them to read, he posed the question: "How did the school get organized around these seven forty-minute periods a day, with students going from class to class?" After researching this question, he writes, "I learned that there is no one alive today who knew anyone who was alive when the decision was made." Chances are, whoever made the decision never expected it to be the last word a half century later.

It is certainly possible to have school with something other than seven forty-minute periods a day. Theodore Sizer's Coalition of Essential Schools, based at Brown University and now involving seventy-eight schools, is working toward a rethinking of the school day and the way content is organized. Many earlier progressives also experimented with diverse variations. Again, knowing more about the history of our work would help us to ask more penetrating questions about the schools and their structures, pedagogical formulations, and purposes.

As a final example, let's consider testing. Because testing is so commonplace, it has been seen as a part of schooling that has *always* existed. But in its multiple-choice, standardized form, it is a twentieth-century phenomenon, a recent development. For example, the Thorndike Handwriting Scale, the first popular standardized test used in the public schools, was produced in 1909. A wide variety of achievement and aptitude tests quickly followed. By the 1960s a majority of schools across the country were engaged in some form of standardized testing but the magnitude was *extremely* small by today's standards. Few people who completed high school before 1950 took more than three standardized tests in their *entire* school careers. And the results of the tests were hardly ever discussed: parents didn't receive the scores, and schoolwide results never appeared in newspapers.

By contrast, those who completed high school in 1990 will have taken, on average, from eighteen to twenty-one standardized tests, and many will have taken many more. To understand the overall magnitude of the shift, we should note that since 1950 the volume of testing has grown at an annual rate of 10 to 20 percent (Haney and Madaus, 1989).

For these 1990 graduates, a considerable amount of attention was paid to preparation for the tests, including many days of completing a host of practice tests. Admonitions about "doing your best" and "how important this test is to you and your school" were common. Those not familiar with contemporary practices in schools would be surprised at how much time is actually spent on test preparation. During these test preparation times, as teachers know well, reading ceases being a matter of real books, writing that matters ends, math stops having a connection to the world, and the arts, if they exist at all, are shelved. Teachers I discuss this with are not pleased about what they are providing children, even as their children are scoring better each year on the tests.

Further, the test scores of these 1990 graduates were the "talk of the town," filling many pages of newspaper space. But these newspaper accounts will probably do more to confuse readers—or confirm their biases—than inform. Proclaiming that *"only* 57 percent of our students at grade nine read above grade level, " they will not explain that "grade-level equivalency" is a mathematical extrapolation and not a reading construct, that half of all test takers *always* score below grade level because grade level is nothing more than the midpoint on a scale, and that the scores might not be useful to teachers or students and might limit the possibilities of more substantive accountability.

Another measure of the changes in testing is instructive. Testing practices, as we noted earlier, began an upward spiral after 1950, and the tests were used more often for selection and retention purposes. But by today's standards, we would consider them relatively benign, at least up to 1965. In addition, before 1965, the tests were not often used in the early grades. This is important to understand. There was a consensus associated with the traditions that gave rise to the kindergarten, and to the subsequent developmental beliefs guiding the primary grades as a whole, that the early years were "special," a time for natural growth and development. Where serious testing programs existed, they generally began in grade three or grade four.

Then after 1965, testing exploded, especially with regard to its uses. As evaluation demands grew with the influx of new federal and state resources on behalf of schools, the tests were quickly seen as inexpensive and easy measures for meeting the demands. And with the accountability movement of the 1970s, the tests became quickly the definers of standards in almost all curriculum areas. Yearly testing, beginning in grade three, became more the norm, though in many school districts accountability demands contributed to the use of annual fall *and* spring testing as a means of determining "gains" in achievement. By the mid-1970s, testing started to regularly invade the primary grades. Earlier developmental understandings began to erode. And early years' testing became a growth area. In the 1980s, testing of young children became commonplace. Increasingly, tests are being used to determine children's readiness to enter kindergarten and to leave kindergarten. Moreover, the tests are also being more commonly used for placement decisions, essentially early tracking. The inappropriateness of such testing should be obvious.

My appeal in this chapter is that we need to be more serious historians of education. That is part of what it means to be a professional teacher, a person able to speak authoritatively and confidently about matters that affect children and young people in the schools. Without a strong historical base for our work, we easily lose sight of the social context that surrounds schools. And we lose the potential for constructing serious reform.

Twelve

Strengthening Our
Commitment to Schools

Teaching is a challenging profession with many wonderful aspects. It provides a way to stay young at heart, to maintain a lifetime of active learning, to be a special part of the world of the present *and* the future while having opportunities to delve into the past. It is in every respect a profession of hope.

We are rapidly moving toward the twenty-first century, our third millennium. Unlike those who lived in earlier centuries, we are faced with the possibilities of a spent environment, an ecological Armageddon. Finding a more accommodating relationship with the natural world and preserving resources are becoming ever more urgent. And in a rapidly changing geopolitical and economic environment, the need to construct healthier relationships with all who occupy the earth with us has enlarged, even as the threat of a nuclear holocaust has grown smaller. Education is not the whole of this future and the imperatives that face us, but it is a central element.

In this extended letter I am aware that I have outlined a particular world view of education, one in keeping with many of the hopes associated with an earlier and ongoing progressivism. But that orientation, filled as it is with a belief in the intelligence of teachers and the power of children and young people to be consequential learners, a commitment to democracy, and an understand-

131

ing that parents and communities more broadly must be deeply involved with the children and the schools, is worth pursuing.

I have implied in many ways that the schools are not, for the most part, good enough. Students aren't challenged sufficiently, the materials available aren't particularly rich in their potential, curricula are too narrowly conceptualized, and the structures that dominate schools tend to impede responsiveness to students, families, and communities. I believe we know how to construct better schools. But the commitments to do what is necessary to bring them about are not yet high enough.

There is currently a great deal of rhetoric about restructuring schools. In general, this has come to mean greater decentralization around school-site management, greater teacher decision making, and more community participation in the life of schools, plus a variety of new partnerships involving business, industry, arts organizations, colleges, and universities. We need such restructuring, but we need to place it within a framework of consequential purposes. Otherwise, what passes for restructuring will be formulaic and limited in substance, leading ultimately to greater cynicism. We can't afford that when our educational needs are so large.

Schools are, for the most part, too big and impersonal. Constructing smaller schools, even within already existing large schools, should not be difficult. Yet little of this is occurring. We need to organize a more diverse range of educational structures that are less bound to time and space. Young people should have available to them many more ways of pursuing their education. To continue to construct their education around the calendar and daily time schedules that now exist is to ensure too many losses of opportunity. And the resources present in our towns and cities are too rich to be kept so far outside the educational arena.

While the struggle for a universally generative education is great everywhere, the difficulties are most apparent in the cities. Yes, the dilemmas of urban schools are connected to the seemingly intractable problems associated with poverty, overcrowding, inadequate housing, unemployment, insufficient health care, and drugs—but there are still ways of ensuring that these schools become far better. Why, for example, should children in our cities be in schools so poorly maintained, so shabby? Why should they be in classes of thirty to thirty-five when their needs for personal attention are so profound? Why don't they have well-stacked libraries and working laboratories? Why are arts programs viewed as a luxury? Why must the teachers and principals who are close to children and young people be limited by so many bureaucratic constraints that they have difficulty achieving their best work or maintaining a view of large possibilities? Why must these schools have such limited fiscal resources when compared to schools in their surrounding suburban communities? We need to ask these questions over and over again. And we should not be satisfied with answers that keep the status quo intact.

I do not mean to ignore or minimize needs of schools in our midsize cities, small towns, and rural communities. Children and young people, wherever they are, need our best efforts. But, regardless of the setting, teachers need to construct for themselves a more powerful voice. That is perhaps my overriding message. I remain convinced that we would not have the same external pressures—for accountability rooted in standardized tests, a regulatory orientation to schools governed by persons and groups who stand far away from particular schools and their students—if teachers themselves were clearer and more articulate about their purposes, speaking and writing about their hopes for children, young people, and communities. But it is not impossible to reverse such directions, and it is not too late.

My optimism is based on my experience in schools. I have not been in a school where I didn't meet teachers wanting to reaffirm in active ways the commitments that originally brought them to teaching, and build a more constructive learning environment for their students. Such energy needs to be reinvigorated and actively supported.

In the world of early-twentieth-century progressivism, school meetings were often closed with a ritualistic reading of Walt Whitman's "There Was a Child Went Forth" (Whitman, [1855] 1973). That was a good, uplifting tradition. I close with a few of the lines as a way to remind us, as well, that our work is children.

There was a child went forth every day,
And the first object he look'd upon, that object he
    became,
And that object became part of him for the day or a
    certain part of the day,
Or for many years, or stretching cycles of years.
The early lilacs became part of this child,
And grass, and white and red morning-glories, and
    white and red clover, and the song of the phoebe-
    bird.
....
And the water-plants with their graceful flat heads, all
    became part of him.

And all the changes of city and country wherever he
    went.

His own parents, he that had father'd him, and she
    that had conceiv'd him in her womb, and birth'd
    him,
They gave this child more of themselves than that;
They gave him afterward every day, they became part
    of him.

The family usages, the language, the company, the
    furniture, the yearning and swelling heart,
....
The hurrying tumbling waves, quick-broken crests,
    slapping,
The strata of color'd clouds, the long bar of maroon-
    tint away solitary by itself, the spread of purity it
    lies motionless in,
The horizon's edge, the flying sea-crow, the fragrance
    of salt marsh and shore mud,
These became part of that child who went forth every
    day, and who now goes, and will always go forth
    every day.

Bibliography

Aiken, W. *The Story of the Eight Year Study.* New York: McGraw-Hill, 1942.

American Association of Colleges of Teacher Education. *Teacher Recruitment and Retention.* Washington, D.C.: AACTE, 1988.

Armstrong, M. *Closely Observed Children.* London: Writers and Readers, in association with Chameleon Press, 1980.

Bellah, R., and others. *Habits of the Heart: Individualism and Commitment in American Life.* Berkeley: University of California Press, 1985.

Brice-Heath, S. *Ways with Words: Language, Life, and Work in Communities and Classrooms.* New York: Cambridge University Press, 1983.

Britton, J. *Language and Learning.* London: Penguin, 1970.

Britton, J. *The Development of Writing Abilities.* London: Macmillan, 1975.

Broudy, H. *The Uses of Schooling.* New York: Routledge, 1988.

Bruner, J. *The Process of Education.* Cambridge, Mass.: Harvard University Press, 1960.

Bussis, A., Chittenden, E., and Amarel, M. "Reflection on Teaching." *City College Notes,* Spring 1974, 2–7.

Bussis, A., Chittenden, E., and Amarel, M. *Beyond Surface Curriculum.* Boulder, Colo.: Westview, 1976.

Bussis, A., Chittenden, E., Amarel, M., and Klausner, E. *Inquiry into Meaning: An Investigation of Learning to Read.* Hillsdale, N.J.: Lawrence Erlbaum, 1985.

Calkins, L. *Lessons from a Child: On The Teaching and Learning of Writing.* Portsmouth, N.H.: Heinemann Educational Books, 1983.

Calvino, I. *Six Memos for the Next Millennium.* Cambridge, Mass.: Harvard University Press, 1988.

Carini, P. *The Art of Seeing and the Visibility of the Person.* Grand Forks: North Dakota Study Group on Evaluation, 1979.

Carini, P. *The Lives of Seven Children.* Grand Forks: North Dakota Study Group on Evaluation, 1984.

Carini, P. "Education Values and the Child's Impulse to Value." Unpublished manuscript, 1986.

Carmichael, L. *McDonogh 15: Becoming a School.* New York: Avon, 1981.

Carnegie Foundation for the Advancement of Teaching. *Conditions of Teaching, 1987.* Princeton, N.J.: Carnegie Foundation for the Advancement of Teaching, 1987.

Carnegie Foundation for the Advancement of Teaching. *Conditions of Teaching, 1990.* Princeton, N.J.: Carnegie Foundation for the Advancement of Teaching, 1990.

Center for Teaching and Learning. *Teacher Interview.* Grand Forks, N. Dak.: Center for Teaching and Learning, 1972.

Center for Teaching and Learning. *Staff Development Handbook.* Grand Forks, N. Dak.: Center for Teaching and Learning, 1979.

Central Park East Secondary School. "The Promise." School publication, New York, 1988.

Chittenden, E. "The New York City Science Test." Princeton, N.J.: Educational Testing Service, 1986.

Coles, R. *The Moral Life of Children.* Boston: Atlantic Monthly Press, 1986.

Comer, J. *School Power.* New York: Free Press, 1980.

Cook, A., and Mack, H. *The Word and the Thing: Ways of Seeing the Teacher.* Grand Forks: North Dakota Study Group on Evaluation, 1974.

Council of Great City Schools. *The Condition of Education in the*

Great City Schools. Washington, D.C.: Council of Great City Schools, 1986.

Cremin, L. *The Transformation of the School.* New York: Knopf, 1961.

Cremin, L. *Public Education.* New York: Basic Books, 1978.

Curti, M. *The Growth of American Thought.* New York: Harper & Row, 1964.

DeLima, A. *Democracy's High School.* New York: McGraw-Hill, 1941.

Denzer, E., and Wheelock, A. *Locked In/Locked Out: Tracking and Placement Practices in Boston Public Schools.* Boston: Massachusetts Advocacy Center, 1990.

Dewey, J. *How We Think.* Lexington, Mass.: Heath, 1910.

Dewey, J. *The Child and the Curriculum.* Chicago: University of Chicago Press, 1956. (Originally published 1902.)

Dewey, J. *The School and Society.* Chicago: University of Chicago Press, 1956. (Originally published 1899.)

Dewey, J. *Democracy and Education.* New York: Macmillan, 1961. (Originally published 1916.)

Dewey, J. *Experience and Education.* New York: Macmillan, 1963. (Originally published 1938.)

Dewey, J. "The Need for a Philosophy of Education." In R. Archambault (ed.), *John Dewey on Education: Selected Writings.* New York: Modern Library, 1964. (Originally published 1934.)

Dewey, J., and Dewey, E. *Schools of Tomorrow.* New York: Dutton, 1962. (Originally published 1915.)

Duckworth, E. *Inventing Density.* Grand Forks: North Dakota Study Group on Evaluation, 1986.

Duckworth, E. *"The Having of Wonderful Ideas" and Other Essays.* New York: Teachers College Press, 1987.

Edman, I. *John Dewey.* New York: Bobbs Merrill, 1955.

Education Daily, Aug. 1, 1989, p. 4.

Engel, B. *Handbook on Documentation.* Grand Forks: North Dakota Study Group on Evaluation, 1975.

Engel, B. *Informal Evaluation.* Grand Forks: North Dakota Study Group on Evaluation, 1977.

Featherstone, J. "A Note on Liberal Learning." *Colloquy,* 1988, *2* (1), 1–8.

Freire, P. *Pedagogy of the Oppressed.* New York: Herder & Herder, 1971.

Froebel, F. *Education of Man.* Englewood Cliffs, N.J.: Appleton-Century-Crofts, 1974. (Originally published 1895.)

Fuentes, C. Interview in *Christian Science Monitor,* Sept. 28, 1986, p. 16.

Fussell, P. *The Great War and Modern Memory.* New York: Oxford University Press, 1975.

Gardner, H. *Frames of Mind: A Theory of Multiple Intelligences.* New York: Basic Books, 1983.

Gordon, J. W. *Diary of a Country School Teacher.* New York: Dell, 1970. (Originally published 1946.)

Gould, S. J. *The Mismeasure of Man.* New York: Norton, 1981.

Graves, D. *Writing: Teachers and Children at Work.* Portsmouth, N.H.: Heinemann Educational Books, 1983.

Greene, M. *The Teacher as Stranger: Educational Philosophy for the Modern Age.* Belmont, Calif.: Wadsworth, 1973.

Greene, M. "Wide-Awakeness and the Moral Life." In M. Greene, *Landscapes of Learning.* New York: Teachers College Press, 1978.

Hampshire, S. *Thought and Action.* New York: Viking, 1960.

Handlin, O. *Race and Nationality in American Life.* Boston: Beacon Press, 1957.

Handlin, O. *John Dewey's Challenge to Education.* Westport, Conn.: Greenwood, 1959.

Haney, W., and Madaus, G. "Searching for Alternatives to Standardized Tests: Whys, Whats, and Whithers." *Phi Delta Kappan,* 1989, *70,* 683–687.

Harste, J., Woodward, V., and Burke, C. *Language Stories and Literacy Lessons.* Portsmouth, N.H.: Heinemann Educational Books, 1984.

Heller, E. *The Disinherited Mind.* New York: Meridian Books, 1959.

Hernden, J. *How to Survive in Your Native Land.* New York: Simon & Schuster, 1972.

Horne, H. *The Teacher as Artist.* Boston: Houghton-Mifflin, 1917.

Hull, W. *Children's Thinking Seminars.* Grand Forks: North Dakota Study Group on Evaluation, 1978.

Jackson, P. *Life in Classrooms.* New York: Holt, Rinehart & Winston, 1968.

James, C. *Beyond Customs: An Educator's Journey.* New York: Agathon, 1974.

James, W. *Talks to Teachers on Psychology and to Students on Some of Life's Ideas.* New York: Norton, 1958. (Originally published 1899.)

Jervis, K. *Children's Thinking: From the Seminars to the Classrooms.* Grand Forks: North Dakota Study Group on Evaluation, 1979.

Johnson, H. *The Nursery School.* New York: Bureau of Experiments, 1916.

Johnson, M. *Twenty Years with an Idea.* Tuscaloosa: University of Alabama Press, 1974.

Keizer, G. *No Place but Here: A Teacher's Vocation in a Rural Community.* New York: Viking Penguin, 1988.

King, M. L. "The Role of the Behavioral Scientist in the Civil Rights Movement." *American Psychologist,* Mar. 1968, *23* (3), 180–187.

Kozol, J. *On Being a Teacher.* New York: Continuum, 1981.

Landrum, R. *A Day Dream I Had Last Night.* New York: Teachers and Writers Collaborative, 1971.

Lazerson, M., and others. *An Education of Value.* New York: Cambridge University Press, 1985.

Lean, A. *And Merely Teach.* Carbondale, Ill.: Southern Illinois Press, 1968.

Linscott, R. (ed.). *Selected Poems and Letters of Emily Dickinson.* New York: Anchor Books, 1959.

Lortie, D. *Schoolteacher.* Chicago: University of Chicago Press, 1957.

Madlock, A. (ed.). *The Giraffe Gazette* (official journal of the International Giraffe Movement). New York: The Giraffe Connection, Winter 1989.

Mayhew, K., and Edwards, A. C. *The Dewey School: The Laboratory School of the University of Chicago.* New York: Atherton, 1966. (Originally published 1936.)

Murphy, R. (ed.). *Imaginary Worlds: Notes for a New Curriculum.* New York: Teachers and Writers Collaborative, 1974.

National Coalition of Advocates for Students. *Barriers to Excellence: Our Children at Risk.* Boston: 1985.

National Commission on Excellence in Education. *A Nation at Risk.* Washington, D.C.: U.S. Government Printing Office, 1983.

Naumberg, M. *The Child and The World: Dialogues in Modern Education.* San Diego, Calif.: Harcourt Brace Jovanovich, 1928.

Olson, R. A. *Evaluation as Interaction in Support of Change.* Grand Forks: North Dakota Study Group on Evaluation, 1980.

Passmore, J. *The Philosophy of Teaching.* Cambridge, Mass.: Harvard University Press, 1980.

Patton, M. *Qualitative Evaluation Methods.* Newbury Park, Calif.: Sage, 1978.

Perrone, V. *The Abuses of Standardized Tests.* Bloomington, Ind.: Phi Delta Kappa Foundation, 1977a.

Perrone, V. "Documentation: A Source of Personal/Professional Learning and Staff Development." *Insights,* Apr. 1977b, pp. 1-15.

Perrone, V. *Working Papers: Reflections on Teachers, School, and Communities.* New York: Teachers College Press, 1989.

Perrone, V., and others. *Secondary School Students and Employment.* Grand Forks: Bureau of Educational Research and Services, University of North Dakota, 1981.

Perrone, V., and others. *Testing and Evaluation: New Views.* Washington, D.C.: Association for Childhood Education International, 1975.

Petkau, B. *A Prairie Puzzle.* Altona, Manitoba: Elim Bible Institute, 1982.

Pratt, C. *I Learn from Children.* New York: Simon & Schuster, 1948.

Pratt, R. *Battlefield and Classroom: Four Decades with the American Indian, 1867-1904.* Lincoln: University of Nebraska Press, 1964.

Read, H. *Education Through Art.* London: Faber and Faber, 1970. (Originally published 1943.)

Rotzel, G. *The School in Rose Valley.* Baltimore, Md.: Johns Hopkins University Press, 1971.

Rowland, S. "Classroom Enquiry: An Approach to Understanding Children." *Outlook,* Autumn, 1984, *54,* 48-55.

Sarason, S. B. *The Culture of the School and the Problem of*

Change. Boston: Allyn & Bacon, 1982. (Originally published 1973.)

Sarton, M. *I Knew a Phoenix.* New York: Norton, 1959.

Sizer, T. *Horace's Compromise: The Dilemma of the American High School.* Boston: Houghton Mifflin, 1984.

Stock, P., and Robinson, J. "Taking on Testing: Teachers as Tester-Researchers." *English Education, 19,* 93–121.

Strieb, L. *A Teacher's Journal.* Grand Forks: North Dakota Study Group on Evaluation, 1984.

Thomas, D. *The Schools Next Time.* New York: McGraw-Hill, 1973.

Tobier, A. (ed.). *Evaluation Reconsidered.* New York: Workshop Center on Open Education, City College, 1973.

Tobier, A. *In Louis Armstrong's Neighborhood.* New York: Queens Colleges School Community Collaboration Project, 1988.

Tolstoy, L. *Tolstoy on Education.* (L. Weiner, trans.) Chicago: University of Chicago Press, 1967. (Originally published 1862.)

Traugh, C., and others (eds.). *Speaking Out: Teachers and Teaching.* Grand Forks: North Dakota Study Group on Evaluation, 1986.

Twain, M. *Life on the Mississippi.* New York: Bantam, 1981. (Originally published 1873.)

Weber, L. *The Advisory to Open Education.* New York: Workshop Center on Open Education, City College, 1973.

Whitehead, A. N. *Aims of Education.* New York: Macmillan, 1959. (Originally published 1929.)

Whitman, W. In H. W. Blodgett and S. Bradley (eds.), *Leaves of Grass.* New York: Norton, 1973. (Originally published 1855.)

Wiggins, G. "A True Test: Toward More Authentic and Equitable Assessment." *Phi Delta Kappan,* May 1989, *70,* 703–713.

Wigginton, E. *Sometimes a Shining Moment.* New York: Anchor Press, 1985.

Wurman, R. *Yellow Pages of Learning Resources.* Cambridge, Mass.: MIT Press, 1972.

Index

A

Academic scholars and reform
  movements, 125-126
Accountability: assessments for, 68-
  79, 130; teacher authority over,
  78-79
Africa, burdens in, 3
Aiken, W., 59
Amarel, M., 85-86, 92, 100
American Association of Colleges of
  Teacher Education, 49
Ann Arbor, Michigan, assessing
  writing in, 75-76
Appalachia, ethnographers of lan-
  guage in, 82-83
Armstrong, M., 90
Asian students: immigration of, 6-
  7, 45, 52-53; teachers for, 49
Assessment: classroom documenta-
  tion for, 74-77; theory-based, 76;
  of writing, 72-77
Assessment Performance Unit
  (APU), 71-72
Association to Benefit Children, 44
Australia, assessment in, 71

B

Bellah, R., 7
Black students: experiences of, 45,
  47, 48, 51-52; in special educa-
  tion, 95; teachers for, 49
Boston, Cambodian student in, 52-
  53
Boys' Club, 43
Brazil, economic competition in, 3
Bread Loaf, 15
Brice-Heath, S., 82-83
Britton, J., 77
Broudy, H., 46
Brown University, coalition based
  at, 128
Burke, C., 77
Bussis, A., 85-86, 92, 100

C

California at Berkeley, University
  of: materials development at,
  125; teacher preparation at, 118;
  writing project at, 15
Calkins, L., 73, 77

Calvino, I., 5
Cambodia, immigrants from, 6–7,
    45, 52–53
Cambridge, Massachusetts, curricu-
    lum remembered in, 17
Caribbean area, immigrants from,
    45
Carini, P., 9, 86, 92–93
Carlisle School, approach of, 46–47
Carmichael, L., 91
Carnegie Forum on Education and
    the Economy, 111
Carnegie Foundation for the Ad-
    vancement of Teaching, 123
Carnegie-Mellon University, mate-
    rials development at, 125
Center for Collaborative Education,
    44
Center for Teaching and Learning,
    97
Central American immigrants, 45
Central Park East Secondary School
    (CPESS): curriculum and pur-
    poses at, 13–14, 18; service pro-
    gram at, 44
Chekhov, A., 5
Chicago, University of, materials
    development at, 125
Chicago Museum of Natural His-
    tory, 8
Child study movement, 80, 89–90
Children. See Students
Children's Thinking Seminars, 87
China, People's Republic of: com-
    petition with, 3; immigrants
    from, 45
Chittenden, E., 70, 85–86, 92, 100
Classroom practices, and pedagogy,
    32–33
Coalition of Essential Schools, 59,
    128
Colleges: and evaluation, 56, 59;
    materials development at, 125;
    and teacher preparation, 116, 118
Community, school connections
    with, 38–44, 54
Community Planning Board, 44
Competitiveness, economic, 3–4,
    124

Contracts, and evaluation, 62
Control, and engaging students, 31–
    32
Cook, A., 104–105
Council of Great City Schools, 46
Curriculum: aspects of designing,
    12–24; continuities in, 8–9; and
    "critical thinking," 23–24; and
    cultural differences, 48–52; depth
    in, 16–19; flexibility of, 13, 14,
    54; and large purposes, 13–15;
    and societal imperatives, 15;
    standardized, 83; and student in-
    terests, 18–19; for student under-
    standing, 21–23; and teacher
    interests, 19–21; thematic, 17–18

D

Darwin, C., 36
Day, D., 8
DeLima, A., 90
Demographics, and changes in
    schools, 45–54, 126–127
Denzer, E., 52
Dewey, E., 13
Dewey, J., 3, 13, 17, 29, 34, 50, 85–
    86, 93, 97, 115, 121–122
Dewey School: collaborative in-
    quiry at, 93; thematic work at, 17
Differences, valuing, 45–54
DuBois, W.E.B., 22
Duckworth, E., 10

E

Education. See Schools; Teaching
Educational Testing Service (ETS),
    70
Edwards, A. C., 17, 93, 125
Empowering teachers: and account-
    ability, 77; aspects of, 80–96; and
    authority, 81, 84, 96, 97–109; bar-
    riers to, 82–84; and collaboration,
    93–94; and governance bodies,
    82; and shared inquiry, 93–94
Equity: in instructional materials,
    34; tracking/separation for, 48,
    95–96

Europe: changes in Eastern, 10; immigrants from, 45
Evaluation: and accountability, 68–79, 130; continuous, 62–64; with examinations, 61–62; and grading, 55–67; guidelines on, 59–65; and large purposes, 60; and learning environments, 64–65; and motivation, 60; options in, 60; of student growth, 59–65, 74; of teachers, 65–67; and teaching standards, 112; of writing, 60–61
Expectations: and engaging students, 26, 33; and evaluation, 63–64

F

Featherstone, J., 9–10
Foxfire program, 39
Froebel, F., 7–8
Fuentes, C., 5
Fussell, P. 10

G

Gary, Indiana: community schools in, 127; purposes and curriculum in, 13
Germany, Federal Republic of: assessment in, 71; competition with, 3
Gordon, J. W., 90
Grading: alternatives to, issues for, 58–59; and evaluation, 55–67; history of, 57–58; reflections on, 56–57; and self-worth, 57
Grand Forks, North Dakota: assessing writing in, 76–77; resources in, 41–42
Graves, D., 73, 77
Greene, M., 5, 50, 93, 100

H

Haley, A., 22
Hammurabi, 36
Haney, W., 129
Harste, J., 77

Harvard University: materials development at, 125; teacher preparation at, 118
Head Start, 44
Heller, E., 5
Hernden, J., 128
Hispanic students: experiences of, 46, 48, 51–52; in special education, 95; teachers for, 49
History, curricular issues in, 22–23
Holmes Group, 111
Horne, H., 8–9
Hughes, L., 22
Hull, W., 87

I

Imagination, cultivating, 9–11
Instructional materials: college development of, 125; pedagogical issues of 33–37. See also Textbooks
Intercultural education, 51–52

J

Jackson, A., 124
James, C., 32
James, W., 89–90
Japan, competition with, 3
Jefferson, T., 5–6
Jervis, K., 87
Jewish Guild for the Blind, 44
Johnson, H., 90
Johnson, M., 90
Journal writing, for teacher reflection, 86–87, 101, 104

K

King, M. L., 6, 8, 22, 36, 46
Klausner, E., 92
Knowledge as constructivist, 29
Korea, Republic of: competition with, 3; immigrants from, 45
Kozol, J., 31

L

Landrum, R., 73
Laos, immigrants from, 45
Lao-tzu, 32
Large purposes: and curriculum, 13–15; in education, 5–6, 11; and evaluation, 60; teacher's statement of, 78
Lazerson, M., 9
Lean, A., 10
Learning: as constant, 2–3; continuities in, 8–9, 33; environments for, 16, 41–42, 64–65; resources for, 38–44, 54

M

MacCormick, A. O., 10
Mack, H., 104–105
Madaus, G., 129
Madlock, A., 5
Massachusetts Institute of Technology (MIT), materials development at, 125
Mayhew, K., 17, 93, 125
Merton, T., 5
Mexico: debt burden of, 3; immigrants from, 45
Michigan, University of, teacher preparation at, 118
Morrison, T., 22
Motivation, and evaluation, 60
Mount Sinai Medical Center, 44
Multicultural education, 48–49, 51, 54
Murphy, R., 73
Museum of the City of New York, 44

N

National Coalition of Advocates for Students, 84
National Commission on Excellence in Education, 122–123
National Teacher Standards Board, 111–112
National Writing Project, 15

Native American students: experiences of, 45, 46–47; teachers for, 49
Naumberg, M., 90
New Orleans, reciprocity of teaching in, 91
New York City: curriculum in, 13–14, 18; Open Corridor in, 94; service program in, 44; testing in, 69–71
Nigeria, debt burden of, 3
North Dakota: community resources in, 40; nuclear missiles in, 6; staff development handbook in, 105–109; teacher growth in, 97–98. *See also* Grand Forks
North Dakota, University of: Peace Studies Symposium at, 6; teaching seminars at, 97–98
North Dakota Study Group on Evaluation, 91–92
Noy Chou, 52–53

O

Optimism: grounds for, 133; need for, 10

P

Parents: and assessments, 74, 78; communications with, 88–89; and evaluation, 55–56, 65; as resources, 39–40
Pedagogy: aspects of, 25–37; for attitudes of inquiry, 28–29; and classroom practices, 32–33; and control, 31–32; and instructional materials, 33–37, 125; and student interests, 27–29
Perrone, V., 42–43, 103
Peru, debt burden of, 3
Petkau, B., 6
Philadelphia, grading systems in, 58
Philippines, immigrants from, 45
Philosophy. *See* Large purposes
Piaget, J., 2, 5, 10
Poland, debt burden of, 3

Portfolios of writings, 74
Pratt, C., 90
Pratt, R., 47
Professionalism: of empowered teachers, 80–96; and mentoring, 115
Purdue University, materials development at, 125

R

Reading: from real text, 14, 35–36; by teachers, 15, 93–94
Reflections: on grading, 56–57; in journals, 86–87, 101, 104; by teachers, 85–87, 91–92
Resources: community, 38–44, 54; parents as, 39–40; in service programs, 43–44; work experiences as, 42–43
Revere, Massachusetts, Cambodian children in, 6–7
Rotzel, G., 90
Rowland, S., 90–91

S

Sarason, S. B., 98
Sarton, M., 17–18
Schools: commitment to, 131–134; community resources for, 38–44, 54; disconnected, 38–39; as inquiry centers, 116; restructuring, 27, 118–119, 132; social context for, 15, 45–54, 127; urban, 13–14, 18, 44, 69–71, 94, 132–133
Service programs, resources in, 43–44
Singapore, competition with, 3
Sizer, T., 26, 128
Smithsonian Institution, 8
Social studies, curriculum design in, 20–21
South Africa: changes in, 10; knowing about, 4
Southeastern Educational Laboratory, 113
Stanford University, teacher preparation at, 118

Students: community participation by, 6–8, 38–44; differences valued among, 45–54; engaging, 25–37; garden metaphor for, 8; grading performance of, 55–67; interests of, 18–19, 27–29; language of judgment about, 96; minority, 45–54; observing, 115–116; as primary concern, 25–26; self-evaluation by, 60; understanding by, 21–23; work experiences of, 42–43
Studio Museum of Harlem, 44
Surround for learning, 64–65

T

Taiwan, competition with, 3
Teachers: assumptions about growth of, 100; characteristics of, 117; decision making by, 80–82; development handbook for, 105–109; for different students, 49–50; empowerment of, 77, 80–96; evaluation of, 65–67; group reflection by, 86–89; inservice programs for, 99; interests of, 19–21; as mentors to beginners, 115; multicultural and bilingual, 49–50; professionalism of, 35, 115; public writing by, 90–93, 95, 117–118, 133; reading and writing by, 15, 93–94; as readers of writing, 73–77; recruitment and preparation of, 110–119; refining craft of, 97–109; reflection by, 56–57, 85–87, 91–92, 101, 104; as researchers, 87–90, 104–105; standards for, 111–112; structured interview with, 100–103; student teachers supervised by, 113–115; as students of teaching, 85–88, 97–98, 104, 107; as well known, 20, 27, 30–31
Teachers and Writers Collaborative, 15, 73
Teaching: accountability in, 68–79; challenges of, 131–134; craft of, 97–109; curriculum issues in, 12–

24; differences valued in, 50–52;
evaluation of, 112; as generative,
21–22; historical view of, 120–
130; human things in, 4–5; ideals
in, 5–6, 114; images of, 113; large
purposes in, 5–6, 11; as moral
and intellectual endeavor, 1–2;
mutuality of, 27; pedagogical
issues in, 25–37; purposes and
philosophy of, 1–11; reciprocity
in, 90–92; reform periods for,
122–125
Tests: and evaluation, 61–62; standardized, 68–79; 128–130
Textbooks: and disempowerment,
84, 94–95; limitations of, 30, 34;
and student differences, 46, 52.
See also Instructional materials
Thomas, D., 54
Thorndike Handwriting Scale, 128
Tolstoy, L., 10, 34
Traugh, C., 91, 118
Truman, H. S., 23
Twain, M., 9–10, 34

U

Union of Soviet Socialist Repub-
lics: changes in, 10; knowing
about, 29–30
Union Settlement House, 44
United Kingdom, assessment in,
71–72
Unity, from valuing differences, 46,
53–54

V

Values, generating, 7–8
Vietnam, immigrants from, 45

W

Warnock, M., 9
Washington, B. T., 22
Weber, L., 64–65, 93–94
Wheelock, A., 52
Whitehead, A. N., 5, 16, 34, 35, 38,
50
Whitman, W., 36, 133–134
Wiggins, G., 71
Wigginton, E., 32, 39
Wilder, L. I., 36
Wirt, F., 13, 127
Woodward, V., 77
Work experiences: to Dewey, 121; as
resources, 42–43
Wright, R., 22
Writing: assessment of, 72–77; eval-
uation of, 60–61; in journals, 86–
87; 101, 104; public, 90–93, 95,
117–118, 133; situated, 72; by
teachers, 15, 93–94
Wurman, R., 40–41

Y

Yale University: grading practices
at, 58; teacher preparation at, 118
YMHA, 44
YWCA, 43

ISBN 1-55542-313-2